UNLEASHED

Unleashed
SINA QUEYRAS

BookThug ‡ 2009

Department of Critical Thought No. 2

FIRST EDITION
copyright © Sina Queyras, 2009
Afterword copyright © Vanessa Place, 2009

The production of this book was made possible through the generous assistance of The Canada Council for The Arts and the Ontario Arts Council.

Canada Council for the Arts   Conseil des Arts du Canada

ONTARIO ARTS COUNCIL
CONSEIL DES ARTS DE L'ONTARIO

All rights reserved. No part of this publication may be reproduced or transmitted in any form or by any means, electronic or mechanical, including photocopying, recording, or any information storage or retrieval system, without permission in writing from the publisher.

Printed in Canada.

LIBRARY AND ARCHIVES CANADA
CATALOGUING IN PUBLICATION

Queyras, Sina, 1963-   Unleashed : essays / Sina Queyras.

(Department of critical thought ; no. 2)
    ISBN 978-1-897388-45-7

    I. Title. II. Series: Department of critical thought no. 2

PS8583.U3414U65 2009   C814'.6   C2009-905286-5

‡ Introduction:
To blog or not to blog?

Being a blogger is not unlike living in New York City – you have at your disposal more art and culture and opinion than you ever dreamed of and you are free to partake and engage. In the city you can go out into the grid and attend openings and discussions, lectures, theatre, and so on, often engaging with the person next to you. On the Internet one can go further afield, wander through the Louvre, tap into the Tate Modern, find a donkey farm in Wyoming, a gallery in Whitehorse, a set of data from a mission on Antarctica, trail a cyclist through Chernobyl, find a very local review of a restaurant around the corner.

Navigating the Internet is fraught. One is confronted with excess. And it can be heady. There are programs that will order or disorder or translate one's text. One can find resources, references, pockets of language that can be sculpted, refined, transformed. One can access an author's entire canon, download and reassemble; engage in simultaneous conversations with experts and laypeople about any given subject. And one can do all of this anonymously or publicly. One must be prepared; one interacts horizontally –

and that rhizomatic thinking can be glorious, yes. However, as I argued in an email exchange recently:

> Progress is never clean, never linear, and never cumulative. I now have a paper journal, a Word journal, several ongoing correspondences, my blog, and the ongoing responses to other blogs. Prior to the externalization of my thinking much of that energy went into *one journal and whatever it was I was working on at that moment*...I mourn the loss of that focus, the dispersion of my thinking even as I appreciate the riches of this external, collagist, magpie approach.

What impact does this lateral, ongoing thinking process have on our lives, let alone our poetry? The latter is indicative of the power of the blog – the way that individual thinking can be immediately plugged into a larger nexus of writing and thinking, while remaining firmly embedded in an individual's praxis. The blog reflects all, and leaves a traceable path through time, geography, reading, poetics, and so on.

Blogging is seductive. I write what I want, when I want and publish as quickly as I want. Sometimes this is immediate, which can be frightening because writing is thinking, not just assembling, and it is the matter of thinking that I worry about most in contemporary writing – not just blogs, but other forms of writing. Early in my blogging the ratio of thinking to writing was more even. This is partly to do with New York: there was a lot of walking and riding of commuter trains and subways, which is an essential intermediary, allowing for a kind of spacious thinking that one doesn't get simply sitting at home online. Strangely it seems that the more plugged in we are, the less diversity of thought we have not in what one encounters (although even the Internet can be a very small world if you don't know where to look) but in the physical ways we think — the ways we contemplate, internalize, allow for time and stillness of mind. During my year as writer in residence at the University of Calgary, for example, I did not blog as much. Partly this was due to the decision to focus on a longer project, but it was also because a/ I wasn't seeing enough art and culture to inspire me regularly and b/ I wasn't walking enough. In other words, the ratio of engagement and reaction, rather than production and consumption, was off.

Last winter, my first Montreal winter in over a decade, and second back in Canada, I began to walk over an hour a day through the city. The thinking that occurred on those walks is not reproducible on the Internet. A body moving through space is exercising yes, but also creating mental space so that the thoughts have room to play – that's where my full engagement comes in. Time changes on a walk. Thoughts rearrange themselves, aligning in ways one doesn't anticipate when one stays in familiar routines. All this lateral movement is good, but one really does need to go deep and anchor every once in a while. Of course this alone isn't enough. As sitting at one's computer isn't enough. It's the interplay between worlds, between states of mind, between technology, nature, culture, that makes writing compelling. We can navigate ourselves into the future only so far as we have sufficiently grounded ourselves and our structures in the now.

How we will manage these various forms of communication

and writing might be the great issue of our time. Even knowing what I know about how I work, and how technology does or does not impact my thinking, my life, and my writing, I still find it difficult to manage my relationship to the Internet and to blogging. When is enough? How do I know when to unplug and get out in the world? When is a thought ready to be shared? When am I using up my creative energy and when am I generating it? If we think the matter of fuel is only a transportation related problem, think again. These questions, along with the simple, constant fact of being public, of opening oneself up for criticism, for inappropriate intimacies and so on, is fatiguing.

This question of publicness can't be underestimated, particularly, as my blog posts attest, for women. The question of risk is also a big one, for to think publicly is to take great risks and taking risks means being vulnerable. Experience shows that women are less likely to take public, intellectual risks, less likely to hold forth ideas in a room of men, and the Internet remains a room full of men. In terms of publication women appear to hold their own, but in terms of discussion, of critical attention, and of public discourse around those publications, women's work and opinion of work is still under-represented.

There is the matter of the unstable, or fluid, positions of women. "I might change my mind," is a statement I hear often from women when explaining their decision not to wade into public literary discourse. "If I defend this poem now, I may change my mind tomorrow," or "I'm not sure I've read the poem closely enough," or "I'm not sure I have context to place it in." There is also the matter of honesty: "I'm not an expert," women tell me,

"I'm not sure what I think," or "I don't know enough about…to comment." Most statements reflect a lack of confidence, but also a sense that the way these women are thinking is somehow not "expert enough" to take a public position. Clearly they haven't had the "take a position any position and defend," and the "never explain," "never give in," "never apologize," "take out the enemy" speeches that seem to be at the core of male mentorship, a literary position that linguistically and rhetorically resembles military and criminal law think more than anything else.

In some cases it may be true that one is not well-read enough in a given area – and wouldn't our world be a more productive one if people admitted as much? But it is rarely true that one's opinion cannot be articulated and isn't worth giving, and one's opinion can be built upon, fleshed out, nuanced over time. The ruse of the verbose, all encompassing prose stylist seems designed to keep different voices out of the discussion. There is no "one way" to write and/or think about art or literature or anything for that matter. There is no "one way" to write an essay. Donna Haraway notes the inability of academics to recognize original thought that doesn't come wrapped in the language and rhetoric of their discipline. A language of inquiry, in the sense Lyn Hejinian describes in a book of the same name, reveals a more compassionate and complicated relationship to the self, to the idea under review, a more responsible approach to taking up public space, something we need much more of in all manner of public discourse. Isn't it clear by now that most things are not simple? Have we not yet understood that "either/or," "me right/ you wrong" thinking isn't useful? Are we not yet aware that with so much more opportunity to speak publicly we should be more aware of how we fill that void?

Blogging, perhaps more than any other activity – publication, leading workshops, giving readings – has made me aware of the deeply entrenched nature of the thinking above and the cost of it in our society. The duality is shocking. Rarely do we break out of good/bad, positive/negative, like/dislike modes of discourse. It hasn't cured me of my own tendency toward this – it's deeply engrained in all of us – but it has made me hyper-conscious of my perspective, of the choices I am constantly making. These attitudes and questions nip at my wrists as I type. How to be critical but not negative? How to be open, but also firm, direct? How to be honest, but not overly confessional? (Over-sharing is today's opium.)

It's interesting that we think the way we organize one area of our contemporary lives needs to shift over to new forms but not other areas. The latter good/bad format, for example, one recognizes from journalism – the way our newspapers have been organized, editorials for/against and reports or reviews with a single yay or nay setting the course. Why must journalism's little box-binaries migrate to the Internet? People moved away from newspapers for a reason, and I don't think it was only the technological change. It was also, I believe, wanting not only to hear something new, but to hear some new way of saying and/or thinking.

Sina Queyras
Montreal
October 2009

‡ Timeline:

Pre-phase 13

Phase One 15

Phase Two 71

An Afterword 163

Unleashed: 2004

‡ PRE-PHASE:
An Idea Beginning

‡ Sunday, May 09, 2004

Now she is blogging. Now she is sitting on the black couch listening to the sirens wail and the rain fall. Now she is thinking of oysters. Now she is wondering why this is worth sharing. Now she is thinking, how decipher what is worth reading? Who is to say? Sifters. She thinks we have become a nation of sifters. We dial up and sift through the wreckage. And what is the use of adding one more paragraph to the mother load? She supposes that soon she will find out.

‡ Monday, May 10, 2004

Anne Carson at Hunter. Exploring the fringe Virginia Woolf fingered between something and nothing. 53-minute lecture in praise of sleep in which Carson explores the dream of the green living room. An experience with dementia. "What," Carson asks, "does sleep see when it looks back at us?" And now I have to think of sleep looking.

Unleashed: 2005 | 2006

‡ PHASE ONE:
　The Beginning Begins

‡ Thursday, March 17, 2005
The text is the text is the text

Attended a master class at the Julliard on Tuesday with James Conlon, principal conductor of the Paris Opera. A pleasure listening to up-and-coming sopranos and tenors, and to hear his critique of their performances. Similarities of disciplines: close reading, close reading, close reading. What does the word mean? What is the music saying? Two main themes. One, that the words themselves offer enough clues as to how to sing them, and two, that the orchestration offers what other clues a singer might need. So, pay attention to the word and to the line...good advice for a poet, playwright, or novelist as well. Here are a few of my favourite lines:

> Just in case you were wondering, Mozart does not need pruning...

> Thank you Mr.__ for pointing out the sound of a double t and a double r. The problem is there is neither a double t nor a double r...

‡ Wednesday, April 06, 2005

Suzanne Zelazo has a response to Woolf's *To The Lighthouse*, in *Parlance*. And it's interesting, but for me not as sparkling as other parts of the book. It's a fragmentation of the narrative, and in a way satisfying in terms of its reconfiguring – certainly it's successful, it just doesn't please me as much as the rest of the book does. For instance, the beginning of "Missplit":

> Wetted ashes the body pretends. The flag a
> dismal delirium. Aiming towards empty.
> She falls. How grand after death. Lunation
> toiling monumental impermanence...

Or "Coehill":

> A pyramid in reverse. My echo sees itself
> coming. Hesitation. This is his own hap-
> pening. Make a move and get out of here.
> The delta opened its soft mouth and took
> you in...

Wonderful prose line – so firm. I'm not sure why I hesitate with the "Through the Lighthouse" section. I wonder about the choice to make the fragments so ordered, I suppose. And I wonder too about the coiffed feel of the fragments. More like beach glass than shards, but again, it's a success I would say, a wonderful response to Woolf.

‡ Saturday, June 18, 2005
Kenneth Goldsmith

Was finally able to hear Goldsmith read. He followed two sound poets, the first, Parisian artist Dominique Petitgand, was absolutely lovely. A blend of sound, text, and narrative. Moving and ambient. The second, sound sculptor Michael Graeve, with a dozen or so old turntables, produced sounds that culminated in an experience of feeling like you were in a plane crash.

Goldsmith read from *Fidget*, a day after Bloomsday. Poised, in a white suit with a red polka dot handkerchief and colourful tie, huge ping-pong racket-like sunglasses, hair slicked back. Quite the dandy. His physicality mirrored the text. As he attempted to describe each movement he makes as he is making it, one can understand how the project very quickly became a kind of prison he had to escape from (by artificially imposing an ending – in this case with a bottle of scotch I've heard).

He read from 10 am, 6 pm, and then 11 pm. The last section is the first section backwards, and I'm not convinced about this move.

A note about the location. Issue Project recently moved from the East Village to a most intriguing space over in Carroll Gardens on the fringe between a residential area and the industrialized Gowanus Canal. The site itself has intense sculptural qualities: an abandoned swimming pool, pea gravel, trees growing in odd places, a silo.

The space itself – a former millionaire's love nest – consists of two rectangular columns make viewing difficult, and, well, it's out of the way, and not capable of holding a large crowd. And a large crowd is what would make the space and location workable.

Also in attendance last night was the French performance artist Orlan, who slipped into the silo in the middle of the sound performances, and slipped out again before they were over.

‡ Saturday, July 16, 2005
Difference between poetry and prose

The question of the difference between poetry and prose is a persistent one, and an important one to wrestle with at some point in any reader or writer's life, though why, why does one feel the need to answer it? I'm always interested in finding the edge of whatever genre I'm engaged in at the moment, whether it's a script or a poem. To my mind there is a wide range of writing within each genre, and then a range in between those ranges... Perhaps a better way to say it is, there is "pure" poetry and "pure" prose, and then the wild frontier between the two, except that pure is a dangerous word and tends to elicit protective measures. I could say "conventional," but I suspect any word I chose would be problematic.

‡ Saturday, September 03, 2005
To blog or not to blog

I have considered this question for months now. This project began as a way to share photos with friends in Canada, but with the publication of *Open Field*, it became a place to post information about Canada and Canadian poets and art. In this sense it became – as my friend David Groff suggests – a place to praise and inform. A combination of things I can get behind.

But I've also found that it has become a distraction, a curious leak in my daily focus and practice – whether I post or not, it takes up psychic space. And furthermore, I'm not sure I'm comfortable with the practice of instant publication. What does one expect when one blogs? Replies? Silence? The creation of a community? A soapbox? A journal online? Why put a journal online? Why disperse, instantly one's thoughts? The practice of blogging is central to our times. Everyone is blogging from Rosie O'Donnell to Hurricane Watch to Bloggers for Bush to Viagra. Commercial, political, reasonable and shamefully pornographic, blogs are everywhere. Having said that, I'm still not sure it's a great development. And while I find the impulse fascinating, I'm not convinced I want to take part.

So, with the academic season upon us, this experiment will be winding down. I'm not sure when, but sometime in the next few weeks this blog, with the click of the delete button, will vanish. Instantly. The way it appeared.

‡ Sunday, September 18, 2005
Chelsea this week

ROBERT SMITHSON
Didn't catch a glimpse of Smithson's Floating Island yesterday, my first trip to Chelsea of the season, but I love the idea of this floating barge filled with trees floating around Manhattan. Smithson is, of course, responsible for Spiral Jetty (1970). He was one of the seminal "earth artists" of the late '60s early '70s – recently I viewed his film on the making of Spiral Jetty at the AGO in Toronto. He died in 1973, but this floating island had long been a dream of his. What I want to see is the barge floating down the Hudson. I want to see a chunk of upstate downstate,

season intact...not just a planting for the occasion, a real, living chunk floating down to NYC. Now that would be interesting.

It was a muggy, humid, grey day. Too hot and wet for many folks to be out, but still art thrives. Still we have art on the street, art on barges, art in a travelling moving van. All day I was thinking, as I have been this past year, what is all this fuss about art? I mean I know I love it, I trot myself out regularly to view it, I'm not calling its value into question, rather I'm wondering what function it fulfills not only in our lives, but quite literally in our minds... What is it we're looking for when we look at art? And perhaps more interesting for me to ponder than that question is the question of who, or what, is actually physically, doing the looking? I find myself equally, if not more so, fascinated by the spaces of art and the people in the spaces, how they move and how they look...

KRYSZTOF WODICZKO
If you see something is a fun piece. A projection of scenes that make it seem as though one is looking at intimate moments through frosted panes of glass. One of which was a dog sniffing at the window. Great, I thought, from the outside looking in or in looking out. Either way, it was a reversal that seemed to poke fun at the world of intrigue, the post 9/11 world of "If you see something, say something," which we hear

repeatedly in the subways as people are going about their days, these intrusions sharpen intimate moments.

However, the stories themselves – which I heard only snippets of – apparently each recount an "abuse of power" a "forced confession" of some kind. The artist's statement suggests, "blurred distinctions" between "us and them," real and assumed, etc. seemed less true somehow, or too overtly self-conscious.

LAURIE ANDERSON

Last stop, a new installation by Laurie Anderson titled The Waters Reglitterized – taken from Henry Miller. The Sean Kelley Gallery is at the northern reaches of Chelsea, and requires passing by a taxicab fuelling station and garage. I could have had any one of several dates with cab drivers. It must have been shift change. I have no idea what this would look like but I admit I was pondering the shape of a cab driver date as I entered into Laurie Anderson's world, which may have made for an even more bizarre encounter than usual.

The stills that accompany the show are printed on what seems to be slightly clingy, matte, Saran Wrap™. I knew instantly what she was going for because the night before I had found wide strips of tape hanging off of light posts in Soho and had taken several pictures through them. It was like looking from the inside of a grape (as Woolf described her habit of trying to recreate childhood memory). Anderson's stills are of images from her dreams – the dreams themselves make up the installation.

Stay away from dreams, I was always told, and yet again and

again we come back to them. The question is whether there is anything new in Anderson's investigation? Well, the first thing is her presence in the film. We are invited – and the gallery has what appeared to be yoga mats on the floor for this purpose – we are invited to lie down and either witness, or enter into her nightmares. Or, we can, as she is doing in the film, cling to the curtains at the threshold of the room and peak in. Either way we are voyeurs to the artist's voyeurism. In fact you can see Anderson, on the far right of the photograph, looking on.

Here one encounters levels of consciousness peeled back. Anderson states that she wants to shift her perspective to understand not only her dreams as illusions but also her waking life. Anderson says she kept track of her dreams for months after her tour of the last show (the Moon show). What I wonder is why she chose this dream: a rather pedestrian dream figuring a dead, female body in the centre of a seraglio-like room. An ultra romantic, perhaps primordially victim-centred dream, complete with male gaze (her brother in this instance) and fairy tale fox (not really a fox, which would have been so much better!) set against layers of crimson and other romantic, painterly props.

‡ Sunday, October 02, 2005
Chelsea

If you've ever stared long into a softwood fire — cedar to be precise — you may, as I have, discovered the core of west-coast Native art in the long, thick veins of the burning wood. All is found there: the wide eyes of the masks, the outlines of whales and ravens, the framing of the allegorical totems and sculptures, all in the deep reds and blacks of the embers. The shapes, their roundness, are unmistakable. But most of us are not staring into fires, most of us are staring into screens: computers, TVs, train schedules... And what do we see? A lot of us see Nike, for one thing.

Having gone to high school in northern British Columbia, and played basketball with Nisga'a and Haida high school teams (from New Aiyansh and Masset on the Queen Charlotte Islands), I know how important basketball is to those communities...and how good the teams are.

I had seen photographs of some of the pieces (perhaps in *Border Crossings*?), but even so I was unprepared for the power of them. The tongues and heels of those objects considered sacred to legions of 13-year-old boys worldwide, transformed into masks, and displayed as if they are anthropological finds is, well, moving. Particularly for someone who grew up in and with west coat art. They work incredibly well. There is also an igloo (small scale), made of shoeboxes, and talking sticks made from baseball bats.

Brian Jungen is a complete original. His message so clear and sharp that it pierces. And it's a message that's both timely and resonates beyond its beautiful simplicity. His first solo show here in New York featured a basketball court transformed into sweatshop tables inverting the story of the totemic sports gear to the viewer: elegant, minimal, and intensely realized. I did not have the experience of walking into the room, but having seen this show today I can imagine the effect. Photos of the basketball court and all other pieces are available on the Catriona Jeffries website, though really, this is work that needs to be seen.

There were also two dinosaurs, large and believable in their structure, shape, and scale. But these two are made of out those ubiquitous (and uncomfortable) white deck chairs. You know the kind, $5.99 at Walmart? Who knew they could prove so useful a tool. Must see.

‡ Monday, October 03, 2005
Quote of the day

"I haven't read *Finnegans Wake* and I'm not so sure I read all of *Ulysses*. This surprises even me because I wrote a book about Joyce. The reason I haven't is that I found Joyce too greedy. I have my own life to live." – Mairead Byrne, from Here Comes Everybody

‡ Saturday, October 15, 2005
Edward Burtynsky & Robert Smithson

Everyone is talking about Edward Burtynsky, and for good reason. Burtynsky first came to my attention in *Granta* a few years back. His large-scale photographs of mine tailings and ponds, of abandoned, rusted ships alongside photos of railway cut lines in the Fraser Canyon mirrors a lifelong fascination with the interface of heavy equipment and landscape. How roads slice their way through forests revealing so surgically, the medians rippling like the rough edges of skin after stitches. We are so divorced from the impact of these very basic physical intersections. These can seem benign, but as Burtynsky shows us, they are most often not. And particularly in our time, they reveal not only mass wounding, but also the poison of excess. Not since Robert Smithson has an artist altered our view of the world so dramatically.

Burtysnksy came out of nowhere. Smithson, on the other hand, is an artist who seems so fundamentally present to me that I made the mistake of assuming I knew and understood his work by osmosis. I wasn't prepared to be as surprised and delighted as I was. The Whitney show draws attention to the multi-faceted and wholly instinctive seeming nature of his engagement with the world. A non-academic artist who grew up in New Jersey, Smithson reacted to the space around him, making visible the waste sites and urging others to use them, to reclaim them. It also shows how varied an artist he was, and how important writing was to him. (I can't wait to get into some of his essays, and there are several collected writings…). Finally, it shows how important he was in terms of shaping, not only the whole earth artist movement, but how we think of our physical surroundings. Coming from a state with the largest number of super fund sites in the US, one can see just how urgent his work was/is.

This seems to be what Burtynsky is doing in his work in China – introducing us to a country growing much more rapidly than even we in the west, with our suburban-encroaching notions of development, can imagine. The growth in China promises to dwarf that of industrialized North America – both in quantity and in physical transformation. There are 32 dams being built aside from the Three Gorges Project, which Burtynsky has been photographing over the years. As he points out, "The roads and highways now being built within its borders could circle the equator seven times." One wonders what one has always wondered about the impact of China's population alone, without the impact of this rapid industrialization. Yes, industry continues to arrive in China, but here's Burtynsky from the Saturday *Globe & Mail:*

> …many of these manufacturing jobs are in industries that have been relocated to China from the West, often

for environmental reasons and at great health cost to the Chinese people – such as the waste from the electronics industry. Eighty per cent of North American "e-waste" goes off shore, and ninety per cent of that ends up in China. "Salvaging is a cottage industry," he says, often done by hand in rural communities, resulting in contamination from cadmium, mercury and lead.

The Whitney show really is worth seeing. I especially loved the piece that Andy Warhol once owned: a wedge of seashells from a beach resort in Florida. It consists of three mirrors: one below and two on the sides, fitting snuggly into a corner of the gallery. It is filled with seashells and looks as though it is a mound, although of course it is only a quadrant...the best part is the letter to Warhol on the wall outlining instructions for care. If the mirrors were to break they could be replaced by common mirrors – "they are not precious," but the shells themselves had to be replenished by a pilgrimage to the beach in Florida where they originated.

‡ Monday, October 17, 2005
Life hackers

Intriguing piece on multi-tasking and interruptions in the workplace in this weekend's *NY Times Magazine* featuring one Professor Gloria Mark and her work on soft technology:

> Each employee spent only 11 minutes on any given project before being interrupted and whisked off to do something else. What's more, each 11-minute project was itself fragmented into even shorter three-minute tasks,

like answering e-mail messages, reading a Web page or working on a spreadsheet. And each time a worker was distracted from a task, it would take, on average, 25 minutes to return to that task. To perform an office job today, it seems, your attention must skip like a stone across water all day long, touching down only periodically.

I have to say that I share some of the habits researchers found many of the most prolific and nerdiest geeks shared. One, I use my email as a day-timer. Anything of import, anything that needs filing, printing, etc., goes there first. And two, I simplify by using only one media program, one music program, and no other repetitive devices such as palm pilots, iPods etc. She who understands bookmarking has a leg up. I try to only do things once. I love multi-tasking, but not "repetitive tasking."

Having said that, I've noticed a certain amount of techno-fatigue since acquiring my new laptop, setting everything up, working out the bugs. Wireless is a real drain. Recently I noticed something I'm calling "lost folds." Information gets folded into our systems, but inefficient filing and updating, especially when one upgrades systems, leaves one susceptible to whole slices of one's work/life being lost. As strange as the methods we use to acquire information these days, are the ways we lose it. Strange swaths of information and experience lopped off. Random. Without a trace.

‡ Sunday, October 23, 2005
Quote of the day

About Mrs. Dalloway: "The only good thing to say about this 'literary' drivel is that the person responsible, Virginia Woolf, has been dead for quite some time now. Let us pray to God she stays that way."

Well, at least the book made it onto the list of *Time Magazine*'s 100 all time best novels.

‡ Thursday, October 27, 2005
Overheard dialogue of the week

Students discussing Rutgers Political Science Professor Drucilla Cornell:

> So, every week we read a little bit more about Kant and then we talk, and she riffs, or she riffs, and we talk. Then she goes back to her Kant reading group in the city, which she has been going to for, like, years, and then the following week we meet again and discuss more Kant… She's been reading the *Critique of Pure Reason* for over a decade and you know, she's still thinking about it. I think she tries out her ideas on us, and we respond. It's the coolest thing…

‡ Tuesday, November 01, 2005
Reading Anne Carson

In praise of *Decreation: Poetry, Essays, Opera*

It isn't so much that Carson introduces one to writers they don't know (although she does that too), but rather she provides a luxurious point of entry to writers one thinks one knows. She split Stein open for me and presented her with all the giddy ease of a three-martini lunch.

It was the fragments of Sappho that made me go back to Carson and read her, all of her, with a renewed interest that would develop into full-blown reverence (as it was Carson's use of Stein that made me go back to her and read and reread and reread). How she made Mary Barnard's translations seem so overly tidy and small minded. Now they seem so Poundish, so tightly wound up, so – in a way – dated.

Initially *Autobiography of Red* failed to impress me. Of course, it might have been all the brouhaha surrounding it – I admit that tends to put me off, and if I remember correctly, I was at a residency in Banff and everyone, and I mean everyone, was trotting out their copies at breakfast. And while I admired its freshness, her ability to reverse action and create unsuspecting associations, there seemed to me no emotional core, it seemed all flash and no substance, very self-consciously pomo.

Let's not forget *Short Talks* published by Brick Books in the early '90s. Those prose poems – ontological, surreal riddles, punchy one-liners and jaw dropping perceptual leaps – represent an important shift in Canadian poetry. You'll find a selection of these poems in *Open Field* (which I included not only because I love the poems, but because they offer a sort of bridge between the prose and lyric, because they connect back to Atwood and ahead to the kind of writing I suspect more of us will be doing, because it is the work Americans are least familiar with, and finally because they are excellent). I heard Carson read from *Short Talks* at Sarah Lawrence a while back. She has developed a kind of call and response delivery, and clearly, she is fond of them.

But back to *Decreation*, much of which I have had the pleasure of hearing already. I was at the debut of "Lots of Guns" in New York and witnessed the production along with a night of Stein appreciation that included Susan Sontag and Catharine R. Stimpson, editor of the Modern Library Edition of Stein. I laughed at the "Song of the Lonesome Pine" thinking of Stein with all of those soldiers, those "doughboys" as she called them, and also because there is something so disjointedly, pointedly American about both the song, and the image: the triangles, the "call to beef," the deadpan delivery.

In Praise of Sleep I heard at Hunter College on what I remember as being a rainy, if not moody night, in which I sat at the back of the room and sipped red wine thinking Manhattan a lovely backdrop for Ms. Carson, although the mood was somber and it takes approximately 51 minutes to read the essay.

As Rudman says in his review of *Decreation* in *Book Forum*, Carson seems to have been created by our collective unconscious.

She is a model poet for our times – her cross genre pollination, her ease with the classics, her ability to keep so many "desktops" open at once. She is a Pentium 17, while most of us are still at 4.

‡ Thursday, November 10, 2005
More day in the life of Brooklyn

I live about two blocks from the Atlantic Yards. The site of one of the most contested and potentially devestating/lucrative developments Brooklyn has seen in a century or so. The changes are rapid. Softskull Books used to be on the corner, now there's a showroom for luxury condos – already a half dozen large developments have gone up, more slated. The neighbourhood is still mixed: we're surrounded by treatment centres, Goodwill and Salvation Army stores, but we're on the march. Frank Gehry is coming back to Brookyn to design the monstrosity that will be our undoing.

‡ Saturday, November 12, 2005

Fig, the second instalment of *Goan Atom,* is a transcript of Caroline Bergvall's conceptual and constraint-based poetic practice. I wanted to make an analogy here about poetry and visual art being on opposite ends of the spectrum, but considering the work of Bergvall, such a statement is impossible. While she is in many ways a conceptual artist, her art is text: poetry. The work is multivalent: repetition and variation are often overlaid with graphic, physically performative, or site-specific aspects.

The twelve pieces with prefatory notes, record her concisely crafted performances, each exploring language and materiality. They are not as constraint based as others (Christian Bök and Darren Wershler Henry come to mind) but they are as three-dimensional. Often I feel I'm encountering sculpture when I engage with these texts.

One of my favourite pieces is "More pets." I give you the first section:

>   a more-cat
>   a more-dog dog
>   a more-horse
>   a more-rat
>   a more-canary
>   a more-snake
>   a more-hair
>   a more-rabbit
>   a more-turtle

The poem goes on to complicate itself with chains of words:

>   a more-turtle cat
>   a more-turtle-more-cat dog
>   a more-dog-more-cat dog

And so on.

In "The Oulipo Factor," American critic Marjorie Perloff notes the following about Bergvall's work:

> ...it is derived from post-punk music and sound poetry as well as from literary movements like Oulipo. Her sonic,

> verbal, and rhetorical devices are extremely sophisticated, encompassing Duchampian pun, phonemic bilingual (French-English) transfer, paragram, ideogram, allusion, and found text. In their complex assemblages, these function to explore such areas as our conceptual approaches to female (and feminine) representation as well as the power structures within which these sexualities must function. The doll, the bride, the daughter, the mesh: these participate in any number of games at once sexual and verbal.

I love the description of "sonic" "rhetorical devices" and find the pieces "more pets," for instance, actually unlock whole patterns of language that I hadn't considered. The list of pets and the complications in the rest of the poem provide not only a fresh and heightened interest in the surface/sound of the words but in the associations (particularly when the language begins to bleed from English to French).

"Gong" is the piece I first heard Bergvall perform for Belladonna. This poem is comprised of deliciously slippery phrases: "the girl laughing ejaculates in my hand" "Cixous climbs the ladder of her name." The phrases swirl, grounding us here and there, touching screen, sound, books, commenting on everything from Arundhati Roy to Bergvall's niece's feet.

‡ Wednesday, November 09, 2005
Overheard dialogue of the week

I mean I know this class isn't high on her list of priorities, but I have things to do too, and I have to give them up, so you know, she should at least be prepared...

Yah, or at least dress properly.

‡ Sunday, November 13, 2005,
Chelsea

The Imagery of Chess Revisited at Luhring Augustine is part of a larger show at the Noguchi Museum in Long Island City. The ten chess sets here include work by British artists of Sensation fame – at least three that I recognize but there may be more. But Jake and Dinos Chapman, Damien Hirst, and Rachel Whiteread's pieces were also the most scintillating. The clarity of concept here was so refreshing. Whiteread's meticulously crafted doll furniture (kitchen versus living room), on squares of vintage lino and carpet in her balsa wood game box was delightful. Really, the chairs, the tiny little pots, everything meticulous. She really taps into the colour palate (again, not unlike Georganne Deen) of the '60s and '70s childhood. The penis heads from the Chapman brothers disturbing, as usual, with African Afroed figures against the white, plaited figures shown here. I still don't quite get what these guys are going for with the penis noses and, well, how do you describe those mouths?

‡ Tuesday, November 15, 2005
Overheard dialogue of the week

If I bought that I'd have to buy a new house...

Don't you have an empty wall in your Florida house?

Which Florida house?

‡ Wednesday, November 16, 2005
Zolf & Stephens at Belladonna

As promised, a very brief note on the Rachel Zolf/Nathalie Stephens reading at Dixon Place. I've had the pleasure of reading some of Zolf's *Human Resources* — a work in progress — and it was impressive on paper, but hearing it, even more so. One becomes aware of the many notes she strikes. Humorous and biting, she exhausts HR speak, folding the banal and oppressive into a fractured, abstract narrative:

The tyranny of subject/verb/predicate is neither emotional nor balance like belly or finger or the accident that no longer looks like a symptom. Any dissemination, distribution or copying is strictly on the receiving end I may be missing something here.

I had read, but never heard either Zolf or Stephens read before, and it was good to hear them together. The work was so different, and yet so companionable.

Stephens' new work is scrumptious. In compact, precise sentences that remind me of Lisa Robertson's *The Weather*, Stephens creates a lyrically fragmented world that is both urban/rural/surreal: "In adornment and philosophy. In rivers' edges and wrought bridges, rusted scaffolding." And "After the wide-angled sea. The tall pines felled. The stones where some sit. The waters seditiously." Stephens' writing is in constant flux, but there is, in all of her work, a very calm centre capable of gymnastic imagery and lucid thinking. Not to mention wit: "I went to Hell./It was the same city all over again."

‡ Thursday, November 17, 2005
Wallace Shawn at Noho

He was ambling toward the door wearing the same green hunter's jacket that he wore at the beginning of *Vanya On 42nd Street* and without thinking, both arms went up, *There he is, I said, the God of theatre!*

Oh, he said, appearing to grow several inches in height as he came closer to the table.

You are Wallace Shawn? For now, I was regretting only slightly, my tendency toward NOT curbing my enthusiasm...

I am.

I love your work.

You do?
And so on...not something I engage in as a rule, but who could resist?

‡ Tuesday, November 22, 2005
Photographs by Jeff Wall, from Tate Modern

Jeff Wall, Photographs 1978-2004 at the Tate Modern

There was something shocking about first seeing Wall's realism at the Vancouver Art Gallery in the early '90s. This kind of social commentary, "The Storyteller," for instance, has since come to seem commonplace, but at the time, it was positively explosive. Perhaps it's because while I was at UBC working toward my BFA in creative writing, I was also working with a population of "youth at risk" and saw the underbelly of Vancouver like many seem not to want to see. Wall's photographs are a kind of testimony: yes, there are people sleeping under the bridges in Vancouver; yes, there are addicts shooting up behind the tulip beds on West Hastings and Burrard and Robson; yes, there are twelve-year-olds out prostituting; yes, the drug problem in Vancouver is out of control; yes, there is plenty of racism in the city. All of these aspects of the city have no doubt multiplied, though I'm not sure how much awareness of them has...

‡ Wednesday, November 23, 2005
Journaling into poetry

There are moments in *Decreation* where I hear Virginia Woolf's acerbic wit slice across the page. This, the last stanza of GNOSTICISM IV, could be an entry from one of her journals:

> At the moment in the interminable dinner when Coetzee basking
> icily across from you at the faculty table is all at once
> there like a fox in a glare, asking
> And what are your interests?
> his face a glass that has shattered but not yet fallen.

Cruel? I didn't think it cruel. Wouldn't meeting Coetzee be a scene not unlike this?

‡ Sunday, November 27, 2005
Women blogging women

Back in September I posted a note that said I was likely going to end my blogging adventure. Clearly I have decided not to. There are a number of reasons why, but the most important one may be – dare I say it – a question of gender. Tired old dialogue that it is, I notice there are not enough women engaged in the discussion of poetry and poetics. Over and over again the voices seem to be male, shouting out about this or that school or lineage...deciding what is important and what not in such confident and reductive tones as to shut out the more cautious or considered voices.

Where, one might ask, are the women? Are there still more men writing than women? I think not. So why are there more men's voices out in the world than women's voices? I have my theories. Look to the deletions, the hesitations, the reflective responses... the women are still out there thinking, their voices not quite up for the often bombastic and instantaneous responses. Thanks to Rob Mclennan, who reminded me of this fact in a post months ago either on the poetics listserv or his blog – I can't recall – but it was a sharp reminder of the need for our presence. Also, thanks to Ron Silliman for a constant consideration of these questions.

With that in mind, and for what it's worth, I will maintain a voice here.

‡ Thursday, December 01, 2005

O Cidadán is elusive but less so each time I come back to it. Here, in a review in *Rain Taxi*, Laura Mullen writes:

> The Canadian poet Erín Moure's new book is so brave, has so much truly lively wit, and is so completely fresh it makes a lot of contemporary American poetry look like dorm furniture from Target: instantly charming and easy to discard.

Not just American poetry, Laura Mullen: poetry. So much of

it built in a prêt-à-porter, add a glass of wine and away you go, sort of way. One can add wine to *O Cidadan*, of course, but one cannot sit back and let the lazy "ah," of closure and "you're fine as you are" lap at one's feet. This, the final volume in Erín Moure's three-volume exploration of language, the body, politics and citizenship, is in fact a dense and complex undertaking, but I would argue it is instantly charming as well.

Like *Search Procedures* and *A Frame of the Book*, and all of Moure's poetry for that matter, *O Cidadán* is not easy to discard. Nor is it easy to digest – on the whole. But just listen to how she begins: "Georgette thou burstest my deafness/woe to the prosperities of the world." Burstest! Woe? Thrown a little? You American formalists out there, thinking of someone like Julie Sheehan are you? No, this is also Moure territory. Like Lisa Robertson, she casts her line as far back as she does wide. And I want to say that the sense of vertigo one experiences reading her is more intense because she's doing it without a net, doing it so far on the knife-edge that one sees below oneself the cavernous abyss of mediocre thinking...of relying too heavily on convention. (I want to come back to this, to compare the experience of encountering history, time and theory in the work of Anne Carson, or Lisa Robertson, next to someone like Moure ...).

I want to think not only about Moure's use of this heightened language, but the experience of it coupled by her decentred "I". By the second stanza the centre of gravity begins to loosen with the phrase, "I am not yet full of thee." Full of thee? A familiar phrase, archaic usage, and yet here's where the content begins to upend expectation; here's where formal investigation takes a sharp turn. Suddenly outside – distanced but intimate, as we see in stanza three ("I tasted and did hunger, where/ thou hast touchedst me I did burn/ for peace") – the canvas of the poem enlarges well beyond the borders of the lyric I. This poet, it seems, can be "full" of something outside, can burn, for something she might never see. Am I making too much of this?

‡ Wednesday, March 01, 2006
Rachel Whiteread at Luhring Augustine

Why is Rachel Whiteread so compelling? Is it the purity of vision? The clean lines? Is it the way she physicalizes negative space? How she sees the potential of nothing? Her new show, at the Luhring Augustine gallery in Chelsea had a Pottery Barn feel to it: shelves of simple two-tone objects. Another feature, seams. A reminder of Erín Moure's attention to this in her poetry. How things are folded in, folded over, tucked. So much of what holds space together is so flimsy. The title of this new show is Bibliography, and in this sense is about containment and containers. Open boxes on chairs, under tables, always as Whiteread does, taking our eye to the place we're trained not to go. The way Whitread physicalizes the negative has a morbid feel. The funereal plaster moulds, solid, sereneness.

The folds of cardboard above, on the other hand, felt to me like elegies for our time. But perhaps this has more to do with my ongoing fascination with impermanence, my childhood of boxing and unboxing. In any case, Whiteread has put her finger on a pulse here, and I've been fascinated by her ever since the Sensation Show at the Brooklyn Museum. Nothing has quite had the impact of Untitled (One-Hundred Spaces) (1995): the resin castings of the spaces underneath 100 chairs, which seemed a kind of towering monument to domesticity, to me, it seemed so female. The full-sized house she did a few years back – I think it was at The Whitney? And then last fall, the chess pieces I posted on here.

Chelsea is archival this winter.

‡ Friday, March 03, 2006
Overheard dialogue of the week

On the train, a father and son:

Why are some wars good?

Because they're for the right reasons. That one was for the right reasons. This one isn't.

What is this one for?

This one is because our president is a moron.

Oh.

(pause)

What about the president who cut down the cherry tree... was he a moron too?

‡ Tuesday, April 04, 2006
Talking about visual/concrete poetry

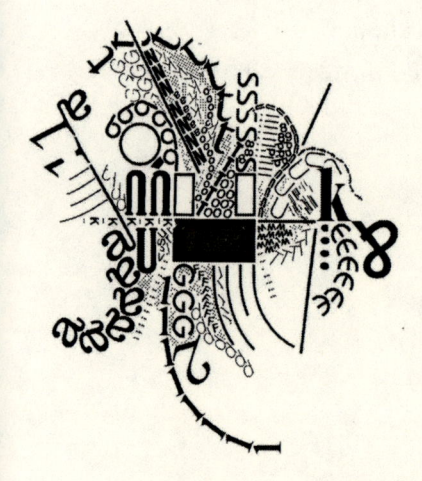

One thing I was comforted by is the notion that this work does not require a "close reading," which I took to mean that it was fine if I showed up ready and willing to engage, whatever I came up with. But when the author states that he is opposed to the reward system around the activity of close reading, I began to worry. All well and good to resist simplistic readings, or systems of reward, but not to urge close reading? Aren't we supposed to be urging folks to look closer? Don't we want people to have strong critical and visual language, to think and interact creatively? But no, I think that the resistance to close reading is a resistance to commodified language, and to specific ways of reading, to specific meaning, not to looking, but rather perhaps that which is too easily ingested.

Now those aren't the same things it seems to me, but I'm willing to accept this premise for the moment and try not to feel stupid for seeing the work so literally. And I feel it's important to do this, to be public about our not knowing, our engaging, our trying out new ways of thinking and writing and being. People are so busy trying to be an expert at something they get defensive, they dig in, and especially as practitioners and instructors of poetry I think it's a good idea for us to be put in the position of reader, of the one responding publicly, the gristly muscle of our minds.

44

"Concrete poetry," derek beaulieu writes, "momentarily rejects the idea of the readerly reward for close reading, the idea of the 'hidden or buried object,'" which it is argued interrupts the "capitalist structure of language." He also discusses the value of silence, though I think not in the sense that Sontag does, though it also resists the idea of commodity, or poetry as commodity, which after all is the most ironic result of the MFA industry. The silence that beaulieu describes, however, is a "poetics of disgust." The poem, in this case the concrete poem, offers what Sianne Ngai terms "our most common effective response to capitalism & patriarchy." Thus the concrete poem is an interruption of value exchange, and on a practical level it offers a moment of silence for those who might acknowledge the passing of meaning.

Pause.

Look.

Suffice.

There is something radical in that.

‡ Monday, April 17, 2006
Art! Brian Jungen, Chelsea

"Thunderbirds" is another riff on the mask, brilliantly conceived in a half dozen rear-view mirrors placed on a gallery wall, each with ghostly white feathers dangling. Part homage to the fluffy dice, part dream catcher, part mask, these mirrors offer an immediate point of entry into the work. Lonesome highway?

45

Northern lights? Descending into the endless road of white culture?

This theme is expanded upon in the eerily soft skulls stitched together from old softball hides and stretched to their max as if running from some unearthly force — more unearthly than raw bone? The garbled soundscape was inaudible to me, but I got the message without looking at the title: "The Evening Redness in the West." What Sherman Alexie did for the short story, Jungen does for conceptual art.

The third installation, "The Evening Redness in the West #1" is saddles that look as though they've been crafted from the slick leather jackets of sports stars, nestled on wooden tables (I thought they were sawhorses, but no). Apparently these move around the room as a heroic battling soundtrack explodes in the background. I couldn't see, and I couldn't stay to watch, but again, a powerful, well-conceived show.

I missed the more playful tones of the transformation masks, but I think the pleasure of that last work was probably a little unsettling. The stark white, stripped down essence of this show hits home.

‡ Saturday, April 22, 2006

I am I because my laptop knows me...

‡ Wednesday, April 26, 2006
3 Penny Opera

The new production of Brecht's *Three Penny Opera* is great fun, much better than reviews would have you believe. Part of this may be, as they say, the difficulty people have with Brecht, but there are some major flaws too. First the greatness: Wallace Shawn's translation is funny, clipped, and in places, inspired. The direction was interesting, but too slow for a modern audience – perhaps it would have been too slow for Brecht's day too, I wouldn't know that. Cyndi Lauper does a kind of Marianne Faithful approach to the songs, which are brilliant, but she's not comfortable in her role of the whore with a heart of gold without the heart of gold. She hits the opening song to perfection, but otherwise appears lost…

‡ Thursday, May 11, 2006
Million Poems Show

Well, I had to check it out, never having seen the show, and only ever seeing Jordan Davis in passing, and being a general fan of his project and poems and photos, I was not disappointed. What a hoot. What Genius. A poetry talk show. There are those who should feel threatened by such tactics, such prowess with a mic, such timing, such mayhem. And Rae Armantrout was a perfect guest. Or are they all this good? Like I said, it was my first time to the show. Who knew poetry could be fun, and mean something too...what a radical idea!

‡ Thursday, May 25, 2006
Richard Serra, The Gagosian

Richard Serra is one of the giants of contemporary art and regularly shows new work at The Gagosian. This latest is more fragmented than the last show I saw: a sculpture tall and curved as the bulk of a ship – one of those lonely rusted ships of Edward Burtynsky photographs. I still don't know how they got that thing in the gallery!

The current show, Rolled and Forged, continues Serra's fascination with weight, density and surface:

> Weight is a value for me, not that it is any more compelling than lightness, but I simply know more about weight than lightness and therefore I have more to say about it, more to say about the balancing of weight, the diminishing of weight, the addition and subtraction of weight, the concentration of weight, the rigging of weight, the propping of weight, the placement of weight, the locking of weight, the psychological effects of weight, the disorientation of weight, the disequilibrium of weight, the rotation of weight, the movement of weight, the directionality of weight, the shape of weight.
> (Richard Serra, 1988)

This last show I saw on a Friday afternoon, which is worth

mentioning because it made all the difference. On Saturdays, the day I usually reserve for Chelsea, the galleries are packed, people spilling, sometimes dazed, out onto the street. Whatever art I might be looking at is therefore shaped in someway by this frenetic energy that I'm viewing it in. This last Friday, however, we were virtually alone in The Gagosian. Alone enough to get a sense not only of the "density," but the surprising warmth, and energy of Serra's pieces. Serra is nothing if not monumental, and I'm never sure how to take his work really, other than with wonder. And respect. Respect for the ability to manufacture something so solid and precise.

Intentional remnants, or pedestals for air, the long steel structures are supposed to "alter and reshape one's perception of space." In Elevations, Repetitions we engaged with the structure as if it were a maze, so one might say that our perceptions were altered. We were certainly aware that something solid was inhibiting and directing movement, as much as we were aware, looking more closely at the structures, that an awful lot of effort had gone in to making them seem so blissfully content with themselves in the air and time. Not the same as finding a massive hulk of steel in a field, for instance, the sadness that rust can bring.

But this is not rust. Not simply rust.

‡ Friday, May 26, 2006
Andrea Zittel

Critical Space, now on at the New Museum of Contemporary Art, is Andrea Zittel's first major show. For over a decade she has been investigating "lifestyle" with more intensity than the average scientific mind. In fact, Zittel might be to "domesticity," what Serra is to a steelworker: the far end of the imagined possibility. Beds slide out of cupboards, as we see in the A/Z Living Unit #21, or the A/Z Escape Vehicle. These are ideas that have lingered around in my mind for some time. Why not have beds that pull out of walls and can be tucked back in? Why not have more compact kitchens, slick ways of recombining storage space with used space? The recycling mind of the Depression era meets art.

Somewhere out on the California desert she is, right now, coming up with new ways of inhabiting space: from daily living, to tuning out, to how we inhabit our own bodies. For anyone who has ever looked at the layout of your average apartment and thought, wow, this is just so wrong, Zittel is your girl. Not only has she thought about it, she has created new plans, and has a gallery to display them...some of which are so tempting you want to make like a gerbil and crawl in.

‡ Wednesday, June 07, 2006
thinking with a small "t":
or the small "t" of missed opportunities

Reading through an old copy of *Line*, the excellent journal out of SFU (is it still running?), in preparation for a post on Daphne Marlatt, I find a series of letters from Charles Olson to Irving Layton of all people... This I found fascinating. Olson and Layton? Who knew. And it made me wonder how Canadian poetry might have developed had Layton been able to get Olson up to lecture at Concordia as early as 1954? What small thinking led to this oversight? Such a missed opportunity. Here is Olson's reply to Layton:

> Black Mountain N.C. (end of March 1954)
>
> Layton
> God damn it. I'm sore. And just becoz I'd set my heart on this thing.
>
> Look: fer chris sake (1) do you have to give it up so easily? & (2) why didn't you damn well let me know at any time previous that (a) it was a Lit Society, & (b) that you were having such other guests as Campbell, Auden & the shit Viereck? [How much do they cost???]

and later:

> how come you find the till empty just now???
> how come the money got spent on
> Auden (Eng)
> Campbell (Eng)
> Viereck (Eng)
>
> By God, Layton. Come on. Come up to it. Or don't, for Christ sake, dangle somebody like me 45 months or more....

Geeesh. How much about the development of Anglo-Canadian poetry does that tell us? But love this opening letter from Olson to Layton:

Mt. Sept 28 53

My dear Layton:

i take you as a sign. The sophistication of yr verse
contradicts yr own cry that, there, sd poet is in exile.
(1) That he is, anywhere, conspicuously in the Northern
American states;
&(2), that at a
certain point of time (end of Renaissance, at least) this
position
makes him leader of any citizen: all are exiled, from a
usable earth

And so a point of connection did not blossom and extend to a larger body of poets/establish roots there in Montreal. All because Louis Dudek "did not like" Olson's verse! Damn the infernal ties with the most conservative strands of British poetry! (Isn't this still the case in Montreal?) Damn small thinking of all kinds. And so a whole other decade before the Vancouver conference!

But what riches we have all inherited from that…thank God the West Coast said yes. Say yes, damn it! Just say yes!

‡ Friday, June 30, 2006

Arbitrariness has to do with a generation which has been brought up on shopping for ideas…– Zaha Hadid

How far can randomness go? When is arbitrary simply haphazard? A particularly juicy topic coupled with community, a word I've been mulling over, an idea, and my expectations of it, I've been examining. I want to believe in the power of communities to affect change in this world. In fact aren't they what makes us citizen and not simply consumer, the consumer the ultimate "I", singled out as the policital and economic kingpin? Robertson suggests that it is individual friendships and not necessarily community that feeds us (or her in any case). As a former west coast entity I haven't yet shaken off the desire for alternative worlds, leaving the grid, architectural independence, the creation of intentional communities. I think of poetry as one of those intentional communities. Perhaps naively.

‡ Saturday July 07, 2006
Notes toward an essay on criticism

Never out of fear
Always with curiousity
Never with spite or malice
Always trying to make connection
Never with your own agenda
Always with a sense of possibility
Never angry at what you don't yet understand
Always mindful of the past

Looking at Pope's "An Essay on Criticism," he says "The gen'rous Critick fann'd the Poet's Fire,/ And taught the World, with Reason to Admire," and why not? Be positive or not at all. Be critical but positive, why not? Criticism can build or dismantle, yes, but even in dismantling, or deconstructing, one can have obliteration in mind, or one can have reconstruction. Why not choose the latter? Why not with a mind to more? Delight and instruct, as they say, rather than piss on and piss off.

There are few nasty reviews that I've found justified. For instance, Kate Taylor's review of Judith Thompson's play *Perfect Pie*, a long while back now, asked a very good question: Why was this play not developed further? Can we not expect more from a playwright of this calibre? As an admirer of Thompson's, and someone familiar with both her work and play development in Canada at that point, I felt the questions justified. Furthermore the reviewer, it seemed to me, was not merely venting her own bias (i.e., she just didn't "like" what Thompson was up to and was never going to "like" it), she was asking for accountability within the greater context of Canadian theatre. Much different.

Pope again:

> Avoid Extreams; and shun the Fault of such,
> Who still are pleas'd too little, or too much.
> At ev'ry Trifle scorn to take Offence,
> That always shows Great Pride, or Little Sense;
> Those Heads as Stomachs are not sure the best
> Which nauseate all, and nothing can digest.

The art of reviewing, is after all, an art. So why not give it the rigour we expect of other forms of art? What I come back to again and again is the language and usefulness. Too much reviewing, it seems to me, is over personalized. My students of writing know better than to preface any criticism with "I like" or "I didn't like" this or that work. Who cares what the reviewer likes and doesn't? Of what value is such criticism? What would happen if critics chose to write from a position of wonder instead? From a position of actively discovering or creating themselves, of being part of building a language (perhaps not a common language, I feel the most earnest of those '70s feminists tapping my shoulder just now) of creation... Not of emotion, not of pitting one's own emotional responses against a nation, but from a conscious position, aware of oneself in relation to the whole, teeming, fragmented, complex, certainly not one thing to any one person no matter how tightly one tugs on the leash...

Leave lover's quarrels for the bedroom...Or, as bell hooks might say, if you say that violence is love, you don't have any idea what love is.

I don't recognize being pulverized as love.

This is, in Brossard's terms, "ill-communication." And perhaps Brossard at her strongest conveys this possibility. A rigorous tenderness. But having evoked the tender, I must also say that I do not desire a noodley reflexive muscle all wet with batted, blind love-lashes...One might love the text, feel pleasure in it, and still maintain a critical stance. Furthermore, one must be able to understand projects that are not their own — in fact that are far from their own. This is, to my mind, what makes a good poet great. Not operating from a place of fear, needing to criticize anything and everything that does not mirror one's own project, but being able to look on differance with an eye of understanding, appreciation, and above all, for what can be learned and applied to one's own work. Moving forward, always, creating more.

‡ Wednesday, July 12, 2006
Lisa Robertson's Office for Soft Architecture

Oh, you just have to love a book launch at Value Village. This event falls under the category of "where I wish I was right now" instead of enduring the smog and 90 degree temperatures of the northeast...but as readers of the Hound will know, Robertson is a favourite, and *Soft Architecture* – published first by Clear Cut Press in Oregon, and now released by Coach House in Canada – is a favourite of the favourite. The essays here read as beautifully as those perfectly fit Levis you can't throw out, simple and elegant. But the simplicity is deceptive. Layers of sartorial and philosophical references, and hours of casual and rigorous thinking make these texts seem light. Surface, colour, depth, historical analysis, and grand walks – not the flaneur we have become accustomed to, the sense of which has been diluted it seems to me, by our constant referencing. The seven "Walks" included here reignite the possibility of walking in the tradition of Stein and Woolf who bring so much to the movement of the language, as well as the seeing itself.

The lustre of headless Barbies and *I Dream of Genie* lunch kits has faded a little (okay, only a little...), but I still get very excited about a well tailored suit, or a particularly sly leather coat. And while the days of filling a cart up with clothes for a crisp twenty-dollar bill have gone, compared to the price of vintage on Queen Street, or the East Village, VV remains a bargain. As for Robertson's book, like *The Weather* and *Debbie*, it's one of those texts you come back to again and again and find something more to delight in. Not "read once" and never feel compelled by it again books. And as far as any object or text is concerned, is their higher praise than that?

‡ Tuesday, August 29, 2006
Elizabeth Willis

Turneresque and *Meteoric Flowers*, both by Elizabeth Willis, who (along with Kate Colby), will kick off the Belladonna Series in just two weeks. And what a kick off. I've carried Willis's two recent books around for a few weeks now, dipping in, dipping in: there are lines in here so good you simply can't move beyond them without pause. And so you pause:

> Such a tree I think is sweeping out this country air…
>
> Idly I turned your name into a kite.
>
> I stain lengthwise all I touch.

For sheer pleasure, for the arch, erotic touch, for the breadth of references packed into each line, I am reminded of Anne Carson, but moreso, Lisa Robertson. And readers will know how fond I am of Lisa Robertson, and of the prose poem in general. Like Robertson, Willis proves my point about its formal flexity (yes, I said flexity), its deceptively simple structures, its lyric capability. Particularly in the era of the autonomous new sentence, as Ron Silliman has suggested, the whole unit shoulder to shoulder, minimal and modern; the one and the many; intimating, stating, inferring, moving the poem along.

The titles of the prose poems are taken from the text of Erasmus Darwin, the text's muse. And what a wonderful thief Willis is, excising gems like "her mossy couch," "grateful as asparagus," "glittering shafts of war," and on and on, each one more gleaming.

As for the lyric interruptions, these also put me in mind of Lisa Robertson – *The Weather* in particular with its dispatches from "Residence At C___." Robertson reverses the notion of interruption, much like Willis has here, and both to great effect, challenging the notion of ragged right-margined poetry, recognizable as couplet, or narrative driven poetry, its tonal sincerity, its accommodating flow.

Here's Willis from "Verses Omitted" – the lyrics that punctuate the Cantos of prose poems:

> Belimbed as a willow
> I'm burning with wingedness

or

> I joy to dream
> a more fortunate planet

Turneresque is, perhaps, a less precise gem than *Meteoric Flowers*, but here is a case in which the less polished, or less tucked in nature of the former, pleases more than the high gloss of the latter. There is something "perfect" about *Meteoric Flowers*. Not a bad fault if one has to have one. But in a time when there is much to say about relative states of completeness, there is an argument here, for a few strings untied. In some ways, *Meteoric Flowers* kind of ode to beauty. There is an edge, of course. But like the boxes of Joseph Cornell – which more than one other reviewer has pointed out – the form is a brilliant container for the disparate object therein.

There is similar energy in Turneresque with its play on Ted Turner's TV world, and Turner the 19th-century landscape painter, and again with its investigations of the prose versus broken line, but much more edge. Thanks to Penn Sound you can hear Willis read from much of *Turneresque*, and you can find excerpts online, including a sonnet sequence on *HOW2* and the final sequence of prose poems titled "Drive."

Here is an excerpt from "Elegy" that gets at Willis's ability to "turn," a trick that drives the poems in this collection:

> The day I drove
>
> in a driving rain
> from realism to impressionism
>
> a moving hillside fooled the town

While a poet might strive for this kind of sleight of hand, not many achieve moves with such grace, without showing the string up the sleeve, the clumsy shifts usually caught up in words "like" or "as" or "such" that expose – and not in a good way – metaphor, or metonymic structures.

‡ Sunday, October 15, 2006
Why you're a painter and you're a poet

Actually, the show I refer to below is called Gurgles, Sucks, Echoes by Roni Horn with a text by Lynne Tillman, which I'll get to in a minute. But first, a timely overlap in that it brings together a curiosity about textual art, Roni Horn, narrative, story telling, and poetry.

I saw the Kay Rosen show at Yvon Lambert last week in Chelsea. The word plays here are representative works: "Jackie-o-Lantern," and "Awning/lawn."

If one is confused about the line between conceptual art and poetry, this exhibit, and the many other textually based works exhibited in Chelsea and elsewhere this year alone, may further confuse. And maybe that's a good thing. These "paintings" in fact do more than a lot of poetry I encounter to make vivid the ludic linguistic play evident in the sounds we utter hourly with so little attention... The sculptural play is actually very layered, though it packs the kind of concrete punch of a slick ad, or a logo, and there is something sweet about the colour play and the perfection of the font, so clean, so precise and so punny. While I hesitate to want to cede that visual artists may be more attuned to a word's verbal and visual lexicon, I must, when confronted, bow to a master – particularly one who takes words back into the community, as Rosen does, literally reconfiguring them in public spaces. This, it seems to me, is something that poetry so often fails to do.

Then there is Roni Horn. The effect of these paintings is like that of the multi-coloured crayon covered over with black and then scratched away. They are lower case and the letters squeeze together often awkwardly.

Roni Horn has the best titles, which are in fact the paintings themselves: "Bending Moments, "Being Purple," "Sometimes Dead," "The Limit of the Twilight is 49 Miles," "Perceptible Includes the Library," "An Old Woman who has passed her life on a small Scottish cliff island is uncomfortable on the mainland because she can no longer see the edge..."

I wonder if Frank O'Hara would still think the same way about painting versus poetry as he did when he wrote, "Why I am not a painter..." I also wonder why this isn't concrete poetry? Take the recent *Shift & Switch* anthology out of Canada that has a large and varied selection of visual and concrete poetry by people such as Rob Read, Gustave Morin, Matthew Hollet, which seems more like visual art than the visual art above. This is a thumbnail comparison of course, and I'm simply wondering here, not making an argument...but maybe what I'm uneasy about or weary of is the articulateness of the above pieces. These are not so much the "inarticulate marks" that bealieau refers to in his concrete manifesto, as they are the articulate pun...

‡ Monday, October 16, 2006
Zhang Huan vs. the Scotch Tape Folks
& After Language Poetry

Chinese photographer and performance artist Zhang Huan has a stunning show up in Chelsea. His work interacts with people, history, geography; exploring the threshold of pain, human and metaphorically it seems, the effect of humans on the planet. The iconoclastic image "Raising the Trout Pond 1 Inch," which has a string of migrant farm workers standing in a pond, speaks to both the cataclysmic and hopeful aspects of our future on this planet for example. Here we see a shot from the series "My Boston" in which the photographer attempts to "enter into" the text in various ways, and below are we gagging on our past? Our history? Can we wash ourselves clean from it or are we awash in it now?

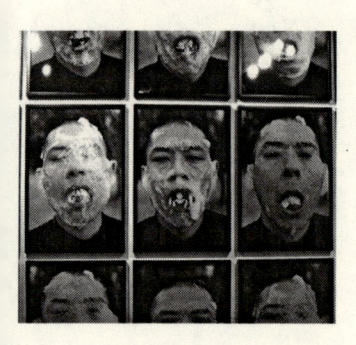

No padding. Like artist Marina Abramović, Huan really does show us the edges, the places where we can see the framework, the more guttural structures that create our world. This is much more interesting to me than other work such as Jessica Stockholder, for instance, who attempts to explore a similar thing with much less at stake. Or perhaps, I'm misreading her focus on the ragged edges of her sculptures – the Scotch tape, the line between paint and object. This gesture, which I've seen repeatedly in Chelsea over the past few years from sculptural work to photography (people tearing out images and taping them together etc.), seems comical in comparison. What have you to expose, I want to ask? What edges are there between the trip from Staples to the studio? Perhaps that isn't a fair comparison, but at least I have figured out what it is about the current Scotch tape movement that bothers me so much...

And does this relate back to poetry? Absolutely. I am thinking of Jena Osman's brief essay "After Language Poetry," which you can read here. She distinguishes between the Aristotelian and Brechtian models and says that the latter is what she strives for in her work. Not that aha moment, that simplistic aha moment that we get to in so much poetry, that "I have wasted my life" or "life sucks but at least I have my porch and I am thankful for it" but rather that "Holy shit, is that what I'm unconsciously doing in my life? My God, maybe I should DO something!"

Or, maybe the writing is doing something?

Or, maybe words have more energy than we believe?

Or, maybe poetry shouldn't be about making the poet feel solid at the centre of the world?

Or, maybe the genius of the artist is her ability to be in a state of unknowing?

Or, maybe the work that interests me is not so much the work that is busy attempting to cement itself into this or that school, but rather out on a limb, quaking with its own newness.

Who are we to believe that we can imagine how literature will behave?

Silly, silly, those who believe they can shape future generations.

‡ Tuesday, October 17, 2006
Why I'm not discussing feminism

Wondering what happens when men speak is a lifetime occupation. All over the globe women with their heads between their knees, wondering. This is an occupation. This wondering. How do men weep? Is it like thinking? When men think is there a little pause before speaking? Why have they not changed the world, men? How many years of thinking and still there are so many problems. Maybe it's time to give them up? After all, men are only one half of the population. Troublesome as they may be. This is why I'm not discussing feminism. This is what it leads to.

Happily words continue to come from other places. There will be no discussing of feminism here. Anyone who wants to discuss feminism should go and read about feminism. Reading about feminism is a way into feminism. Imagining being a woman is another way into feminism. Imagining then, is feminism. Thinking is also feminism. So, there will be no arguing about feminism. After all, what is feminism? Feminism is doing. Feminism is seeing. Feminism is women being and doing. Talking about being and doing is a way to keep women from doing. Really, women need to be doing and not thinking of ways to explain to men what it is to be a woman. Men need to explain to men what it is like to be a man, or to be a woman, or to be a stone, and they must try to do this without hurling, or spearing, or other means of combat.

Who is invested in having women not doing? Suddenly everywhere people are thinking. Wow, that is what doing is. And now there is a lot of doing. And suddenly there is a lot of trying to arrange the doing into schools of doing and hierarchies of doing which is a way to assert bigger doings over small doings. But meanwhile women too are doing and they are not always good at doing in order. Therefore unruly. Therefore in need of reining in. Therefore in a big corral.

Still, if everyone is doing then men therefore are women if they are thinking and women are men if they are doing and everyone is feminist if they are seeing. So if looking then feminist. If looking is seeing. If you look and what you look at looks back, not you looking back, then feminist. Naturally things are more complicated than they seem, and naturally, quite naturally, it is time for tea. *STFU*

‡ Sunday, November 05, 2006

crimes against humanity no fish in fifty years crimes against humanity six women killed in Iraq crimes against humanity is good for the Iraqi people crimes against humanity sentenced to death by hanging crimes against humanity in Beirut crimes against humanity in Iran crimes against humanity is crimes against humanity is no fish in fifty years is blind eyes and blind eyes is crimes against humanity what are crimes against humanity stay in bed for humanity stay in bed for humanity read newspapers for humanity write letters for humanity who hangs who for humanity who kills who for humanity i don't understand humanity i am not fond of humanity i want humanity back i want to believe in humanity i am not understanding of this humanity i am all over this humanity where is humanity hanging for humanity war crimes against humanity is bones is humanity is confused is humanity is the bill coming soon who will pay the price for humanity and fish and fish and fish and fish and don't confuse fish with humanity and don't confuse humanity with humanity and it is time to unplug and walk it is time to unplug and walk while we can still walk while we can still walk while we can still walk

‡ Friday, November 24, 2006

I've been thinking of other ways to use the time I would normally use blogging. I'm convinced that there are more effective ways of being at the moment. Particularly as it seems that while I sit here typing (even now), whole species are becoming extinct and with the same zeal that folks have wiped out much of the old growth trees and stripped resources and polluted water bodies and soil and air in North America, the entire globe is being developed at a rate that makes my head spin...how to take all of this in?

Meanwhile our world becomes smaller under the guise of being more global...we come to our screens in the morning but what are we looking at? Most often it seems to me we are looking at ourselves. And poetry? Well, as much as I believe in poetry and will obviously always engage in it, I worry about an art form that seems to have completely accepted the idea that it is only talking to itself.

This poet wants to talk to non-poets as well as poets. This poet wants to hear good news about the human race. This poet wants to see some hopeful signs for the planet. I'm concerned about gender and power and poetry yes, but like so many other things, water, global warming, I generally feel hopeless about it. Meanwhile there are people who are putting their foot down, who are really seeing what the implications are of us allowing the privatization of our water sources, the dislocation of local in terms of water, and what that will mean even five years down the road.... Who would have expected this stance from a Christian organization?

One of the most inspiring people I've ever heard of is a man whose name I don't remember. He's a man who, when forced to retire from his work due to a head injury, began walking daily in Toronto's Don Valley. After a few days he began picking up garbage. Then he began to bring bags with him because he found so much. Then he began recording what he found. Then he began looking further into the land around him and began discovering bigger things, shopping carts, televisions, etc., which he diligently hauled out and recorded. Then he began to talk about it, then he began to get attention, then more people became involved and ten years later the Don was suddenly showing signs of revitalization... I love that story because it's a great reminder that dailiness adds up. That "heroes" are usually the most common people doing common things. That there are signs of hope. Real, not virtual. Real.

And I suppose in the face of this a daily blog is harmless enough. But I want more than harmless. I want to shift things. I want to shift. What would I have after ten years of blogging?

‡ Wednesday, November 22, 2006
Winding down

After much consideration, I've finally chosen a date to pull the plug on this adventure. Lemon Hound will officially end along with this turbulent year. Hopefully I'll be able write at least mini-reviews of all those books I have stacked by my ugly orange chair. What's next? Indeed. What's next?

‡ Tuesday, November 28, 2006
Overheard quote of the week

What do you mean I have the wrong kind of ant farm?

‡ Tuesday, December 19, 2006
More musing on the idea of blog

I said in an earlier post that I think one of the downsides of blogs and blogging in general is it seems that we pay less attention to actual books. I still think that's true...as Noah Eli Gordon suggested recently at Kelly Writers House, the danger of blogs etc., is that we get caught up in the cult of personality rather than the poetry...that seems a danger no matter what the venue, but I agree on some level.

I do think that blogs bring attention to books that might otherwise be missed. I know people email me to say they heard of this or that book and have found it, and so on, and I know I've heard of poets and books that I wasn't aware of through other's blogs. And these books might not be reviewed in mainstream venues, so how would one necessarily find them?

On the other hand, I wonder if people are still paying attention to print journals. Or, do we assume blogs will take the place of such traditional reviewing venues... Do we need print journals?

Another, even more disconcerting aspect of blogging for this writer is that the idea of public has entered into my workspace. This is not good. My laptop is wireless so pretty much wherever I am, I can be online, I can be connected. This has many benefits – but I'm not sure discussions about poetry is one of them. It makes for little distance. It flattens the process, makes visible, and while collaborative thinking/writing might be exciting, for this writer, it needs to be one part of a whole range of things, and there needs to be much more alone time. Suddenly that's difficult to achieve.

Unleashed: 2007 | 2008

‡ PHASE TWO:
The End of the Beginning

‡ Monday, January 01, 2007
Happy New Year and so long...

Now that *Time Magazine* has dubbed the Internet person of the year we might think the age of blogging is over. Isn't that what it usually means when mainstream media crowns anything? And of course neither *Time Magazine* nor Lev Grossman can be faulted for yet another representation of the Internet..and the blog...as a male space....can they?

Oh, how many times I bite my tongue. It's boring, boring, boring...and non-stop. And yes, I know they added pictures of female bloggers...cheerleaders and knitters.

After 18 months of blogging I find myself scattered, my thoughts fragmented, my sense of the world strangely off-kilter, and I can't help but wonder the timing...maybe it's better to view the world through the limited scope of the blogosphere? Maybe we can't handle what's happening out there in the real world?

In any case, I'm off to bury my head in books, and in the world of brick and earth and scent and rain, and hopefully to see people in the flesh, poems, art and music in hand. Happy New Year. I will post upcoming readings etc., and I hope to see you in person, on land, sometime in the new year...or perhaps in another incarnation.

‡ Tuesday, March 27, 2007
Just 7%

The percentage of art in the Tate Modern produced by women. This is not the National Gallery, not the Louvre, places where such percentages might not necessarily raise an eyebrow, this is the Tate...this is modern.

‡ Saturday, April 28, 2007
Narcissism is all the rage, remix

> We do not lack communication. On the contrary we have too much of it. We lack creation We lack resistance to the present. — Deleuze/Guattari,

Nothing is new in photography. Well, not the mirror image, and really, how can you beat yourself for a subject? You're everywhere you go, you're evasive, mysterious, yet endlessly willing, endlessly fascinating, a constant storm of expression and desire, moving through the city like a great wind. Photography, Susan Sontag pointed out in her essay "Plato's Cave," has become a right of passage, a "social rite, a defense against anxiety, a tool of power." This pre-digital essay responds to the already ubiquitous camera, now even more so, and surely soon to be grafted onto the human body. She points out that the family album has become an essential document, and in fact what is missing is often more noticeable than what is not. We need evidence of participation, or presence, and idea that has taken us to ridiculous extremes – sending photographs of each other over dinner at the same table, for example.

But what Sontag didn't anticipate was the extent to which these technological advances in photography would turn our gaze back onto ourselves. Not only can we google ourselves endlessly, luxuriating on our own cyber-markings, we can now photograph ourselves doing it and publish that instantly. What are the implications of all this self-portraiture? A self-absorption that comes with the territory is inflated by our technology, not necessarily by choice. The new Macs, for example, with their built in cams make explicit the idea of our laptops mirroring us. It takes little effort to chronicle our every mood because everywhere we look there we are.

Is this a "resistance to the present?" I can't see that. Technology, and I'm not sure that it's inherently so, but technology seems to take away so much agency. I am aware of this every time I try to make an independent decision with my software, for example. Posting on forums and threads relating to the software affirms my worst nightmare: software designers are control freaks – what we, the end-user, is left with are carefully selected choices. "The thinking has been done for you," they boast... as if this should make one cheer.

A worrying trend, as I've pointed out here before. What are we witnessing here? Is this part of a bid for agency? To see ourselves in control of the technology that increasingly shapes our lives. Is the world expanding or shrinking? And what of our minds? And what of our sense of self? Are we being trained for a virtual existence? As David Levis Strauss points out, "it's not that we mistake photographs for reality; it's that we prefer them to reality."

Furthermore, what is the relationship between the increasing citizen preoccupation and reliance on technology and the domination of market forces? How can one be concerned with dailiness when one is so busy staring in technology's mirror? Democracy, corporation, propaganda...and self-absorption. Have we yet come out of the cave, or are we still being distracted by reflections cast on the wall by the very flames that purport to warm and guide us?

‡ Monday, April 23, 2007
Jeff Wall at MoMA

"Storyteller Looking at Storyteller," The Met, NY 2005

I've written about Jeff Wall before – a brief mention of his show at the Tate Modern last year, among others. After seeing

Wall's most recent show at MoMA in New York last week, I realized that while I've been posting these text-less childhood landscapes since I pulled the plug on my daily blogging, I missed writing and thinking about art. I also remembered that this blog really started out as a way for me to record and respond to the abundance of art I was experiencing in New York, Vancouver and Toronto over the past decade – not necessarily, or only, about poetry or the poetry world. So, it's fitting then, that I come back to the blog now with one of my favourite artists, one whose landscapes inextricably overlap with my own sense of landscape, so much so that I don't know where my memory ends and his work begins...whether I see Vancouver through his eyes, or see him through my sense of Vancouver.

Wall has been making pictures since the early '70s when, after a brief time in London where he received a research degree in art history at the Courtauld Institute, he returned to Vancouver and began making the light box mounted transparencies he is best known for (see above). The transparencies are large, painterly reconstructions of famous scenes, with attention to the mundane aspects that signalled contemporary west-coast life at the tail end of the resource-based economy. The subtext to the images is neither necessary, nor evident to an untrained eye. There was, and is, clearly more here than meets the eye, a notion that has become increasingly apparent as Wall has become more commanding in his work, expansive, and narrative, always with a great sense of anthropological and social witnessing.

The cinematic quality of Wall's work has grown as the technology and, perhaps, the intertextuality of his inquiries grows. He often describes himself as a cinematographer – evoking a sense of movement. Filmic movement. What's particularly intriguing about this idea with Wall is the way he uses frames. Each large canvas is made up of smaller images, meticulously "sewn" together. So the narrative works on the surface of the image, but the frames come together to create a whole image. A completely different idea of "film," "frame," and movement.

Works such as "Dead Troops Talk" (1991–2) and "A Sudden Gust of Wind (after Hokusai)" mimic a photojournalistic style, but they are also strongly reminiscent of 19th-century art and offer compelling critiques of disassociative modern living. Like fellow Canadian photographer Edward Burtynsky, it is partly the scale of the work that is so pleasurable and reassuring. There is simply something absolutely confident about taking up so much space and to do so with historical depth. In a style that others – Gregory Crewdson or Cindy Sherman – would help make uncomfortably familiar by the late 1990s, Wall's staged portraits, his reconstructions, called into question the assumptions of realism.

When I first discovered Wall's work at The Vancouver Art Gallery in the early 1990's I was struck by several things – size, light, scale, of course, but also his refusal to omit. This notion of "including everything," is now virtually cliché, but the combination of grandeur, locale and absolute witnessing (the tiny blade of glass, the turquoise bread bag clip), was stunning to me then and now. There is a tenderness to it as much as it seems "mean." The size was daunting too. In fact, I remember a fellow photographer I was attending the gallery with suggesting a kind of grandiosity – photographs should not be that big, nor should they resemble advertisements, the kind one sees in light boxes in malls... But of course, Wall was taking back that size, composition, and image from the advertisers who had sanitized and enlarged ourselves in unobtainable ways.

"The Storyteller," with its harsh depiction of Vancouver's Downtown East Side, was one of the first images I had seen that didn't "pretty up" the skyline, that seemed, in fact, to amplify the devastation as much as it honoured the subject and subjects. Such subject matter, if covered at all, was usually done in a kind of voyeuristic way, with expectations of "pity" or "empathy." "The Storyteller," does neither – though as one critic points out Wall's images often "reveal" as much as they "veil." And the "Storyteller" honours this idea of sharing, of narrative, and again, of inclusion. Social documents are often chronicles – as fellow Vancouver photographer Lincoln Clarkes shows us with his collection of images, *Heroines*, about the drug addicted women of the Downtown East Side. Wall is certainly part of a burgeoning west-coast photography scene that includes major figures such as Stan Douglas, Roy Arden, Judy Radul, Kelly Wood, and a vibrant conceptual scene showcasing the likes of Brian Jungen, he is also the leader. I should add that his influence is not only felt on the West Coast, and that perhaps he has done more than anyone to make Vancouver's mercurial beauty internationally known.

But back to this idea of veil, which in Wall's world is more about tantalizing than obscuring. And by tantalizing, I suggest that in his view the most arbitrary settings on the planet can be scenes of great triumph and beauty as much as devastation and bewilderment. "The Drain," for instance (which I don't recall seeing at MoMA alas), shows us two young girls on a summer day standing on stones in front of a large culvert – where the water is coming from we're not sure and where their innocence is going we're not sure either, but it is certainly going.... But practically speaking, in those days Vancouver still had many open ditches and drains, and this sense of the world's arteries erupting, as sexuality, as the darker shades of life erupt in puberty, seemed somehow emblematic of suburban childhoods in the late '70s and '80s. These images, if nothing else, made the Vancouver Art Gallery show significant for me, and I've never forgotten them. Here was a much different representation of west-coast life than I was accustomed to seeing in any print or visual media. Take the recent Fred Herzog exhibit at the VAG, which offers spectacular Kodachrome images, historically and culturally important, but predictable in composition and subject matter.

The show at MoMA – which was at the Tate last fall – is fairly comprehensive, with many of my favourite images – "Eviction Struggle," "The Drain," "A Sudden Gust of Wind," "Storyteller," "Mimic," "Milk," and "A View From An Apartment." All are online thanks to MoMA, and are accompanied by notes from the artist. Having seen several shows at Marian Goodman over the last year I had already processed the shock of the smaller, abstract images, the composition of barren spaces – a bar of soap, an octopus lying on what seems to be an old cannery washing board. Images such as "The Flooded Grave" (1998 – 2000) are photomontages, as discussed above, and as such one can see the seams where the image has been collaged to make a whole. This technique, as Wall points out, has largely been about deconstructing images, but here we see it being used to maintain a sense of whole. "Experimental Traditionalism," Wall calls it.

One image I hadn't seen before was "Morning Cleaning: Barcelona," a luscious modernist reverie, reflected somewhat in the face of this woman:

A study in lines, both the simple modernist lines of the architecture and furnishings – contrasted by the veined marble, arranged to intensify the patterns, creating almost alien like shapes. It takes a while to see through the window washer's soapy film to catch the sculpture of the naked woman in the courtyard fountain. "He seems to love the sweepers," my friend said, and there is truth in that. "Someone has to mop up the mess of the world." And this is an important point, and one that the west-coast photographers seem to have in common – a sense of social responsibility, not a hermetic world (à la Cindy Sherman), or an overly sexualized world (Gergory Crewdson, Mike Kelley), but always a working world – whether the work of sweeping, "Volunteer" (1996), or restoring, "Restoration" (1993), or simply surviving, as we see in "Tran Duv Van" (1998 – 2003) – over and over again, the regal quotidian – and that offers more hope than one might initially feel when encountering Wall's world.

Perhaps the most stunning image for me was also one of Wall's most recent. "After 'Spring Snow,' by Yukio Mishima, chapter 34" (2000 – 2005), is a master class in lighting and reminds us that the beauty of the light boxes isn't simply technical or gimicky. Beyond the light box, Wall applies light in delicate strokes. The hair, the buttons on the back of the dress, the gold bell (is that a bell?), these are so reminiscent of 19th-century realism it's impossible for one – no matter how close you get – not to imagine brush strokes. This is lighting at the most controlled level. "Delicate, narratively suggestive, opulent... " I read somewhere that it takes Wall a year or more on average to do a photograph, so perhaps now we'll see even more work and of larger proportions. How rare and fabulous it is to see a huge, mid-career show such as this then, and be left with a tingle of excitement about the work to come, and if "Spring Snow" offers a glimpse of new direction, so much the better.

‡ Tuesday, May 01, 2007
Andreas Gursky at Matthew Marks

Panoramas, bird's eye views, the single largest photograph in the world containing 80,000 brightly dressed gymnasts, a chain of islands, or lines of asparagus plants...the sheer amount of modernity is killing us. It's our unwieldiness that compels photographer Andreas Gursky, featured in April's issue of *Modern Painters*, and on view soon at Matthew Marks. Or is it the money? After all, this is the photographer whose print "99 Cent," sold for $2.48 million. What was the subject matter? The interior of a discount store. Multiples of the lowest of the low.

So, it works. Or we're curious. Or both. Consider "May Day V," with its reverse panopticon effect: everyone is seeing out. Seen next to "Beelitz," which could either be a close up of some kind of cardboard, or a metal door... More than ever, we get a sense of the scale at which we humans are currently operating in: too many choices, too much information, too much to see, too much to process, not a hope in hell of remaining on point or conscious for any length of time. And meanwhile the world progresses beyond what we can possibly remain even remotely informed about...or oriented to. What's up with this road in Bahrain? Is that a mirage? A track? And just where is James Bond Island?

More and more we see photographs tracing the impact of the impact of man in multiples, repetitions, the large scale manufacturing of civilization. We are in love with our own sense of production. And why not? Despite Baudrillard and Benjamin, our sense of being in love with replications – of ourselves and others – goes back a long, long way. Think of the Terracottta Army, Easter Island, etc. But this scale? This abundance? What are we to make of all this? When we see images, such as the James Bond Islands, are we to think of its inevitable disappearance? Or are we to think of the shapes and colours, the surface of the image? Are we to consider the original at all? Do you see a whale, or 8,000 pounds of product? Do we see cow, or skirt steak? Do we see a canyon, or a place for our SUVs? Are we to feel a sense of joy at the discovery of such a view, such a world, or are we to mourn that once we are seeing this replication, the real is that much closer to absent.

Still, there is something extremely compelling about the scale and depth these photographers – Gursky, Burtynsky, Hofer – achieve and the tenderness, the depth of feeling that one senses in the composition, tone, and subject matter. Prefacing Irish writer Edmund Burke from 1756, critic Alix Ohlin suggests a contemporary sublime, a time in which we are faced with "terrible emotion," "terror" and "transformation." Scale. Remember the guilt with which people referred to 9/11 as such, the "brute beauty," if you will, of the destruction? We aren't so much trembling before God, Ohlin suggests, as we are trembling before the sheer presence of ourselves. Difficult to disagree.

And finally, though one can't help but be happy about recent leaps in printing technology, on top of digital imaging, what we are looking at, what we are taking to be documentation, is in fact manipulation. In fact, this seems to be expected now. Ohlin suggests that "to show globalization as it really is – to make the invisible sublime – the image must be altered." Ironic, the technologoy we create to track our technology can't contain or adequately document it.

Finally, there is the suggestion that Gursky presents "our ignorance magnified." While I agree with this assessment, I can't say that this is necessarily a new thing. It seems to me that since photography's invention, it has been an intensified mirror, always offering this possibility to those willing to read the surface and beyond.

‡ May 04, 2007
Looking for, and Resisting, Diane Arbus

I've posted on Diane Arbus very briefly after seeing her show at the Met, and after a show in Chelsea. Briefly, I suppose, because despite her dual giantess status in both the feminist and photography worlds, I'm still not sure what to say about her. The prolific photographer worked extensively in the '50s and '60s, publishing in *Esquire* and *Harper's Bazaar*, showing her work sporadically before committing suicide in 1971. Her work, as I mentioned after seeing her show at the Met, is almost overly familiar. The Manhattan women, the lipstick and high hats, the Puerto Ricans on the street, the hopeful, and fulsome bodies of New Yorkers parading past her lens, all of this seems woven with seminal New York City images of that era. But her body of work, concerned largely with the carnevalesque – twins, outsiders, transvestites, dwarfs, giants, people with Down's syndrome – resists any kind of assessment and fails in some way to convince me of any authenticity...of what? Experience? Art? Intention? I'm not sure, and I'm not sure that it's even a fair criticism, but it's where I am with Arbus. What are we to make of all these faces, similarly blank and otherworldly in expression, like short confessional narrative poems with their minute, repetitive and ultimately cloyingly assuring endings. We are all the same, we are all of us freaks, I am you, you am I, and so on, and yes, in theory, yes.

Perhaps this is what makes "The Twins," so popular. The image, the first Arbus image I recall seeing, satisfies on basic formal and narrative levels: children, doubled, mysterious, a couplet, accessible, suggestive, bite-sized, not overly complicated but resonant.

Looking into the faces in the Arbus book, one sees a vast array of people in various moments, fleeting, caught in acts. But to what end? Are we looking at the straining gaze of a good girl longing to get out of the constraints of privilege? Is that interesting? Looking at her equipment, her library, bits of her writing over the years, in the show at the Met, didn't prove helpful. She had a gift for "rendering the familiar strange," she "uncovered the exotic in the familiar." Arbus's legacy of photographs is impressive, and her influence undeniable. That doesn't make it any easier to engage with her work, or to come to terms with its impact. In some way, Arbus is a collector, and the captures evoke fissures, odd disjunctures that the Walls and Shermans of the world went on to work into a lather of texture and technical wonder.

The child with toy hand grenade, for instance, is an image that had Wall seen and been intrigued by, he would have painstakingly recreated in a way that fully exploited the formal, classical, and contemporary elements; he would have staged a performance.

I'm not advocating one approach over the other. I'm admitting that there is something about Arbus' work that doesn't ring true to me. Judith Butler sees an intriguing thread in Arbus' work by focusing on her depictions of the human body in its urban setting, the figure as it moves in and out of light. I can work with that, the human body, perhaps, as ubiquitous and unsettling as light moving across the city's surface?

Okay, to be fair, seeing Arbus' equipment and notebooks, her library, and family photographs, one gets a sense of the artist's struggle. The hurdles of gender unearth themselves, for instance, glimmers of difficulty, an unwillingness to perhaps put the children first...signs that for women developing a grand, life long project on the scale of a Jeff Wall or Edward Burtynsky is much more difficult. (Hence Virginia Woolf's satsifaction that Vanessa could be mother and painter, but not mother, painter, and terribly successful or famous.) And those who do, Cindy Sherman, Nan Goldin, Candida Hofer, have somehow slipped through the net of likability and expected wholesale emotional administration. As feminist as a man can be – and I know there are men who are feminist out there – I can't think of many who don't rely on the free work (emotional and otherwise) women do to make the world inhabitable, and who do women turn to for that?

But as a whole, Arbus' body of work slips past me. There was a moment when the images seemed to have meaning, as a young girl, but that hasn't lasted. Like Sharon Olds' work, which in the 1980s inspired legions of young poets to cough up images of grotesque penises, make the unmediated psyche their canvas, the poem's surface rippling with managed rage, Arbus inspired students to photograph the liminal – taking their cameras into night clubs and strip clubs, nursing homes and hospital wards, into bath, bed, shower, everywhere the body goes, the lens follows. As a project, for some reason, its luminescence eludes me. Nan Goldin on the other hand, but that's another post.

‡ Monday, May 21, 2007
Rae Armantrout, Next Life

At first glance it seems impossible that there is a Rae Armantrout in this bustling and overwrought, environmentally devastated century, in this overcrowded field of poetics, in the high and ranging ring of "project." So clear are the lines, so airy and delighting in self awareness that one assumes they must come from a Dickinsonian hermit, holed up somewhere – very possibly in the last Redwood in a mall parking lot in California – peering down at us with a cutlass and an eyepiece.

My first Armantrout encounter was not unlike this. Here is a singular voice who seems to be both of the moment, of something much larger and grander, and yet something more simple, and clear, and still – what an amazing feat, still, contemplative, connective, kinetic:

Anything cancels
everything out.

If each point
is a singularity,

thrusting all else
aside for good,

"good" takes the form
of a throng
of empty chairs.

Or it's ants
swarming a bone.

I am reminded of Erín Moure's direct and verbal sparring, her leaps and dives, the word collages, the layering, the uncontainable imaginative force, what seems like a total lack of self-consciousness. How does one measure such things? I'm thinking piercing, no hedging, the arrow on, our near the bull's eye pretty much every time. No lazy thinking here.

Armantrout does what so little poetry does these days — it goes for the heart of the matter, it embraces a complication most of us will do anything to avoid, and it does it with such clean angling that for a long moment, we think we've understood, or not understood, or are perhaps on the verge. It doesn't clear things up. An unsettling place to be. And, of course, exactly where we all are.

‡ Monday, May 21, 2007
Quote of the week

I don't have a problem with lyric poetry. I have a problem with the idea that lyric poetry is the only legitimate poetry....

‡ Sunday, May 27, 2007
Joshua Clover, The Totality for Kids

The Totality for Kids is a thoroughly modern text, written, as Judith Butler suggests on the back cover (as if that isn't "sign" enough...) "in the shadow of Adorno." There be theory in this text; this text be shaped by theory, in both subtle and unsubtle shapings. The presence of an index, for example:

> Adorno, Theordor W., 3
> Agamben, Giorgio, 23
> Alduy, Cecile, 30
> Alphabet, 11,21,36,66
> Anarchasim, 51,52,64

and so on...with more than a dozen references to architecture, cities, money, Paris, suburbs and sun respectively. This is a smart text, an engaged text, a text with reference, a text with relevance, a text embracing high and low, a text which plays with the idea of text – the starburst poem "Ca Ira" (30), and the playful "What's so American about American Poetry?" which appears in both French and English (the French being decidedly sexier):

> Au fond c'est fait au sable.
> Heuresment, parce que sans ça, c'était un véritable casse-tête.

French culture and language are obviously major factors in this text, but it's a different engagement than other American poets (Alice Notley, Marilyn Hacker, CK Williams...), who spend a good deal of time and/or live in France. Clover's engagement is more filmic, more architectural, more Lisa Robertson than the above, but also more Clover: "The sun tutoyers me! Adrift beyond the heroic realism/in the postmodern sublime where every window can lie/Like a priest..."

I took a dozen poetry books (Canadian just for interest sake...) down from the shelf and flipped through, looking at word pairings. Of the ten I randomly chose only Margaret Christakos and Darren Wershler-Henry compared for freshness, for condensed meaning. This wasn't a study, just a random take, but it's worth considering the number of surprising pairings in a text because to this reader in any case, this can be a mark of a text's velocity, its fuel, or conflict (if conflict drives narrative perhaps combustive language drives poetry...).

The city, its shape and structure, its interaction and movement with people and ideas is at the core of this text – not surprisingly Benjamin, flaneurism, etc. But the city exists more acutely in contrast, and in context, rather than narratively (as with Dionne Brand, for example) or formally (as we see with Marilyn Hacker). In that sense, Clover achieves a grandness not by the cliché of the particular (cliché in our insistance, not in its effectiveness), but by the particular view, the angle and rawness of the included particulars, the wide swing from city to suburb, abstract idea to tender moment: "Two boys in a doorway tending each other's wounds," we get in the poem "The Dark Ages," which knocks around the idea of poetic history, form, discussion of the "lamplit" corridors of poetry, where like a magician Clover turns, and turns and turns ideas and images on themselves, offering connection after connection as the narrator moves through space ending at:

> some town square and the strangers look at (him) as if (he) had done something terrible, an otherwise good man who commits murder after murder to understand why exactly he did it the first time.

I've been reading this book along with Judith Butler's *Giving an Account of Oneself*, in which she asks, among other things, how one can go about doing just that in an ethical, honest manner (what is ethical, what is honest?). In the chapter "Against Ethical Violence," she suggests that one's ability to accept what is "contingent and incoherent in oneself may allow one to affirm others who may or may not affirm one's own constitution." This ability to accept, not limitations, but impermanence and growth, not only makes for more accepting humans, it makes for a more collaborative and open textual experience. There are no conclusions in Clover's text. We aren't affirmed in our humanness like so much contemporary poetry tends to do – no lifelines dangling, no balm, no pat endings. Nor are we left unaffirmed necessarily. Rather, we are left ruffled, tousled, having stood briefly at a corner slouched, perhaps thinking of a cigarette, or considering the inherent sexiness of cities meant for people, not cars, having arrived too early, or too late, or maybe not even sure we're at the right address...and its our ability to be open to this that is affirmed if nothing else. Clover achieves a casual balance between OxyContin and "poetic prose." New "sensations" do emerge, and new perspectives. In his hands that seems an easy thing to do. Alas it is not.

‡ Thursday, May 31, 2007

Disobedience was a problematic text for me, one which I picked up, put down, picked up, put down. It seemed, as Fred Wah did when I first encountered him, incredibly hermetic, disinterested in readers. But persevere I have, and remained open, and as usual, was rewarded. *The Descent of Alette*, in fact, is a poem that unlocked whole layers of poetry not only in Notley, but in others. Is it too intimate to suggest that a poet may have such complicated encounters? That not everything is easily or immediately accessible? That sometimes a poet needs to put another poet aside for a time, and that this putting aside need not be a final word, or a judgment on either party as to obscurity or skill, or limitation? In a world so concerned with achieving and defining genius, or "award winning" status, it is rare for people to discuss these matters. And I think to our detriment. Someone suggested to me that I had been introduced to a particular poet backward: "That's not the way in," he insisted. But is there a right way to approach any poet? Can I not come in backward? Sideways? With two other poets on my arm? Standing on my head? Underwater? Can I not come in with a yelp? With a moan? Twice failed and a third time suspicious, but willing anyhow?

It seems to me that entering into Notley's world is a kind of reawakening of voices long ago suppressed, put into storage with the bad cotton frocks and faux fur vests, with the menstrual cups and earth shoes, of owls and a belief in women as something other than – the kind of event where you could shout "Feather!" and half a dozen women would rise. This constant negotiation of gender, of public/private spaces, of polis as a place women skirt, is something we have come to take for granted in this young century, though I'm not sure why. Notley begins her brief essay "The Poetics of Disobedience," in this way:

> For a long time I've seen my job as bound up with the necessity of noncompliance with pressures, dictates, atmospheres of, variously, poetic factions, society at large, my own past practices as well.

Which makes me think that these questions are indeed quite relevant – in fact urgent.

Who is taking on war more powerfully:

> "In this moment" "before" "anyone, ever" "died" "before we were born?"
> "in this moment forever before" "before we went to war"
>   "Before we died" "In this moment, now" "In this moment before, it is
> not before"

or directly, as here, in "White Phosphorous." This poem being the precursor to *The Descent of Alette*, perhaps the most moving poem, the most dramatic accomplishment I've read in some time. The breathlessness, an aspect of women's poetry that has been explored by many (Dionne Brand's *No Language Is Neutral* comes immediately to mind). The full force of the lyric impulse here is momentum – and perhaps the lack of it in *Disobedience* is what made it difficult for me to enter. I have similar difficulty with Leslie Scalapino whom theoretically I admire, but poetically alas (and as yet in any case) don't enjoy. But *Descent*, like Robertson's *Debbie: An Epic*, takes on grand themes and makes them extremely relevant, moving through Dante's underworld, set, most appropriately, in the subways of New York, where the poor and women burn, writhe, and are forgotten, looking for "the father," and ultimately, with the help of earthly, feminine aids, battling "the man," and offering the reader, a brief bit of light in an otherwise, depressing – if believable – epic.

> "There is no darkness" "or light, here" "But when I leave you" "you
> will be lit – " "even if the light" "does diminish" "We were silent"
> "awhile;" "then I spoke again:" "'I'm at peace with" "being" "In
> this moment" "I've become" "all that" "I am" "I'm ready" "to
> go back'"

What is it about *Disobedience* I found so difficult? It seemed, at first, to be a kind of poetry of anecdote and fragment. Each shard, in and of itself, luminous in a way, and certainly interesting:

> The French call
> homelessness, unemployment "l'exclusion."
>
> ———————————
>
> Who do you exclude he says
>
> and I was just thinking "It's better to let her squirm first."

this from the poem "Red Fish," which begins simply:

> but I've changed something...

and in retrospect it's a mystery why something feels elusive at a given point in time –

‡ Saturday, June 02, 2007
Notley's Disobedience and the disobedient reader

After a discussion with Jena Osman on how a poet's modes of writing can shift, it seems a little less mysterious to me how a poem or a poet can appear on the one hand so distant and hermetic and then suddenly completely open and engaging. It sometimes seems that I am the only poet who has these difficulties – either that or people/readers/poets are just not able to admit their own difficulties and the need for growth. Easier to say this or that poem or poet is bad, not playing fair, doing something nonsensical. Revealing, of course, an unwillingness to let oneself sit in the discomfort of not having fit a text into its appropriate slot.

As we were talking, I kept thinking about how the reader had to be a kind of locksmith, sitting in his or her bed at night, or at a table, hunched over a coffee, listening to the tumbling of ideas, willing one's own thoughts or interpretations to achieve a click of meaning... Are great works of art a refraction immediately, or subtly recognizable? How archaic to consider "great works of art," how naive. Or is it?

Osman is one of the most intelligent poets writing today. In the tradition of Leslie Scalapino, Susan Howe and Joan Retallack, we find her creating hybrid texts that are essay, criticism, conceptual art and poetic. See her recent essay in *Jacket*, for example. There is little argument in the face of texts by the above writers that language is a site of urgent political activism. Here is Osman:

> The linguist George Lakoff has argued that we need to unpack and recontextualize the big metaphors behind political rhetorics. Phrases like "rogue state," "friendly nation," and "just war," are based in narrative frames that remain static (some people are good, some are evil, taxes are bad, etc.).

The more intense the dualistic/simplistic thinking, the more important that work. Here's Retallack: "If complexity is the source of our freedom, it is also the source of our terror."

And more and more complex things become, which means that the right-wing business maven Theodor Drucker was, not surprisingly, wrong, when he said that the skill one will need most in the future is knowledge. The ability one needs the most is the ability to think, to handle that knowledge. Fast. We are, after all, only as good as our systems can process information... how many desktops can you have open at once? At what point do ideas begin to blur? Is this part of why suddenly facts don't mean anything? Why people like Bush and Harper can simply say, another set of facts please, those ones are inconvenient...

Disobedience is both lyric and initmate, a kind of epistolary flaneur's account of walking and thinking the streets of Paris – a tradition itself among American poets and impossible not to want to hear Stein's pounding on stone. But this is not Stein, no, this is thinking of a different order, and as Brian Kim Stefans points out in his review of Notley, this text represents a melding of different modes of writing and thinking, a turning point in a way for a writer who moves through clearly defined projects. So, we get from *Descent of Alette* to *Alma, or The Dead Women*, by moving through this intertidal zone where ideas meld and shift, open and close as the mind washes over them:

> Love in caves are love.

> It all
> I mean, the universe
> it had to
> it is a universe of exactness.
> The god we are in is exact.

What is so frightening about thought?

‡ Monday, June 04, 2007

As Ian Davidson points out in his review of *Grave of Light* in *Jacket*, "the trajectory of the poems in this collected work can be read as Notley's movement from this private domestic space in the early work to her broader relationship to public space in later poems such as *Descent of Alette*." Indeed, if such a journey is a prerequisite for a poet, it's even more so for women who, like Alette, must in some way slay the burden of interiority (my computer reads inferiority) and all of the weight that brings, both directly (yawn, yes, that means the domestic sphere) and indirectly (i.e., the expectation that even as a woman might be at the table, she is likely the only one, and is often the receptacle for human emotions and egos even if she isn't responsible for clearing up after and serving tea...).

Such statements as the latter are career suicide, end of story. No one likes a verbose feminist. We like them demure, witty, buttoned down if we like them at all. Believing that we live in a just and enlightened world, women have been conditioned now to tuck feminism so far down in their back pocket that it hits their ankles, perhaps reminding them of the pernicious divisiveness of the female presence (you are, after all, allowed at the table, now don't go spoil the meal, as Edmund White said over a glass of white wine...one doesn't want a bore at the table).

And yes, yes, who wants a bore? After all, after all, things are all well and well – never mind what they are! That the *Paris Review* still can't hit a percentage of more than 25% women writers being interviewed, or the Tate Modern can boast no more than 7% women artists and check out this statistic out of Hollywood – in film, the percentage of women writers of features has hovered between 17% and 19% since 1999. White male writers still make up 72% of guild membership. When women do get a job, they tend to make less money: the median women's earnings decreased 6.1% while make earnings increased 16.1%. Further, I hazard to say that there are few women who have the power of chronicling literature, of ordering it, as the Bernsteins, Sillimans, Wahs, Olsons, Duncans, Creeleys, Lehmans, Geddes, Patersons, etc., of the world do. To be fair, many women I've spoken to have said that such ordering, such canonizing, is not something they are interested in doing...so why whine? Fair enough. Still, it's the world we live in and so at least acknowledge the terms and implications.

Such is the risk Notley takes in her work; all of her work, not only her grand epic. Throughout the collected works we see the impact of gender: we move from poetry that dialogues with children, to husband to philosopher to politician and so on. We are privy to conversations between poets, admonishing gender's limitations, and so on, and we can but cheer as Notley just keeps moving forward, weaving whatever is at hand into her ever-expanding engagement of body with world, making particular the statistic, in unflinching terms. Here, in "As Good As Anything," from *Mysteries of Small Houses*, for example:

> Is there a right and wrong poetry, one might
> still ask as I patronize,
> retrospectively, the Iowa style,
> characterized, as I remember,
> by the assumption of desperation
> boredom behind two-story houses
> divorce, incomes field, pigs,
> getting into pants, well not really....

at which point the poet interrupts herself with "God this is bitchy..." before going on to describe how "You can fuck/a visiting poet: you can be paraded before/ a visiting poet as fuckable but not fuck," and so on. Refreshingly honest in a poetic economy that is as much about "fame" and "fuckability" as anything else, though of course the poem itself is making fun of "the poem" itself.

Does she really say that? Yup. With as much candor as Atwood did in her early poetry, and Anne Carson does today in *Beauty of the Husband*, "The Glass Essay," *Decreation*, and so on. Though one reason I might have found a book such as *Disobedience* difficult to take in the first instance, coming to it coldly, without the warming of *Alette*, is that lack of lyric, that lack of imaginative or refracted leap. The world is more headlines and cut lines, the ongoing dialogue of self with world. I prefer the more lyric poems, the poems that move outside of the commentary on poetry and the poetry world. For though I take certain delight in having someone "name" what we all experience, I find it depressing in truth. It's much more satisfying to be taken far away from such concern – if not in content, then somehow in form, or perspective. Even if that far away is another kind of harsh confrontation. And so much of Notley's work makes that leap.

‡ Thursday June 07, 2007
Nibbling in other fields, 2

How We All Swiftly, Signal, 2005

There is much to like about Coles. The work is accessible, personal, deeply nostalgic and smart. The earlier poems have a kind of innocence, but that gets complicated as Coles progresses. Complicated in his own way, not in the way of Erín Moure, or George Bowering, or Fred Wah, or Robert Kroetsch, or Dionne Brand...but in his own way. Important to remember, I think, that what one might think of as complicating doesn't mean the same thing for every poet. For instance, an early poem begins:

> alone this morning here
> in this cottage where you lived
> the careful last summers of your contracting lives
> rows of rain falling from the eaves,
> the rain barrel irrelevantly filing
> and the disabled wooden sawhorse
> upended years now...

nothing new there, either in language, linebreak or sentiment. For me the best moment is the leap from "contracting lives" to "rows of rain." A fine poem, just not enough happening on other levels, aurally (so much of lyric poetry today gets by with having no lyric quality at all!? How is that?), linguistically, or even imaginatively. But this takes care of itself as the poet progresses:

> There is a narrow endless place
> where the earth has frozen. On this
> they live at unbelievable speeds

or from "Old Sunken Ships,"

> The modesty of them! An hour's flashy hubbub
> and then such endless disavowal
> such embracing of failure, only
> ribbed sand in shadowy re-establishings and
> little frills of water...

or

> I sang. Bullshit. Not 'sang' –
> semaphored. And only when I was
> in the mood...

the last nugget from the final section, and this reader's favourite of the book, titled, "Little Bird." Here the poet composes at unbelievable speed, as if he'd just found a sheet of ice, vast and clear, and wholly untouched. Much energy! An energy we see throughout, but not with such vigour or focus, or perhaps unselfconsciousness – it goes! I was flipping back and forth, noting the break out of one kind of constraint (the emotional narrative waterfall, as I like to call it), and the invention of another, and wondering what precipitated it: had Coles had a sense of this late career breakthrough?

‡ Wednesday, June 20, 2007
In conversation with Zoe Strauss

SQ: My partner and I were talking the other day about how architecture can be so oppressive, how even a street has a psychology, and sometimes, you can't put your finger on it, but there is a kind of psychic dis⁄ease in a random place.

ZS: Oh yes, absolutely. There's no question, and sometimes it's intangible, but it makes a big difference. Like ,in South Philly we have overhead electrical wires and it's oppressive…if I were ever to move from South Philly that would be why because it's like you're literally under a weighty net… And there is all different things that make the feeling of, either the illusion of openness or closure… Once I read in *The Moviegoer* by Walker Percy about walking and how the "new" houses seemed haunted. Something resonated with me about that.

SQ: The new houses?

ZS: Yes, it's not about the history it's about the psychology.

SQ: Interesting. On the other hand, you can take a place that seems totally abandoned, lifeless, and to most people, terrifying, and infuse it with absolute joy...but there's a lot of weight that goes with the territory of being a social documentarian. Particularly of a place like South Philly where you can feel, in some areas, the tension is palpable. And the desperation is really evident block to block. Sometimes it seems you're in a war zone.

ZS: It's really block to block. My block has in the last couple of years become gentrified, but yes, you can go one block and it's... yes, it's like Dresden.

SQ: How do you negotiate that?

ZS: That kind of dichotomy is fascinating because we live with it. That's our lives. It's not an abstract concept of this block is bad, this block is good; it's very difficult to see and think about, but we're all living our lives together at the same time. There's no separate. People have these perceived ideas that this block is this, and this block is this, but it's the same fucking block! You're in the same neighbourhood. For their own sanity, people have a tendency to compartmentalize because we're so packed in like this...and sometimes I think that's healthy and sometimes not. I mean just to get by we don't have to talk to every neighbour, but you need to know your neighbours and you have to be able to interact with them...
<...>
SQ: Influences include Dorothea Lange, yes, but what about Diane Arbus? Nan Goldin?

ZS: Cindy Sherman...Tina Modotti. I'm a fan of all of them. Even if my own interest is unrelated to their work... they're working within a very different framework, a patriarchal framework of who decides, you know, the gaze, and so on. I'm just like, go for it, go be your bad self. You really just have to put yourself out there for people to look at. It takes a lot of effort to put yourself out there – and pushing the work past the point where people will look at it. I mean it's an enormous effort to get past the Jeff Koons' set-up of what we think art is...

SQ: 7%. Did you read that statistic? Only 7% (or 12% more recently...) of the artists in The Tate Modern's collection are female.

ZS: Are you kidding me?

SQ: Modern.

ZS: We're post-post-feminist, post, oh, we've made it. Like we're a Virginia Slims ad. Fuck you. (Just for the record, I'm a radical feminist, and I believe that we're still in the process of creating a feminist movement. I believe the idea that social movements are fixed or static is false, and we're as connected to Seneca Falls as much as we are to Tribe 8...)
<...>
SQ: In an interview with Jeff Wall I noticed recently that he said he had begun to think that the idea of subject no longer mattered. What do you think of that?

ZS: Are you kidding me? What are you saying? I have little

104

tolerance for that...not that process, or theory doesn't matter, but when it comes right down to it, "it" has to be pretty fucking strong to say that the "subject" doesn't matter, and that the theory and the process are the finished work...that's not a judgment on his work, but you really have to be on solid footing if you're going to say the concept is more important. Did you see his show?

SQ: Yes, I know what you mean. I'm a big fan.

ZS: Yes, me too. That piece with the papers blowing in the wind is mind blowing, but to say that the subject...

SQ: Well, yes, I thought so too. And the extent to which the images are reworked and manipulated...

ZS: For me, something gets killed in the process.

‡ Tuesday, July 10, 2007
In conversation with Stephanie Fysh

SQ: To my mind, the *Rooms With Woman* series continues your architectural exploration, further complicating it by including a female figure – yourself – engaging with both the space, and the photographic technology. In a review of that show, Bryan Partington notes that "constraint breeds creativity." I would say that it also creates freedom. There is great clarity in the gestures of these photos, and great energy in the series. Does this series represent a moment of artistic self-discovery?

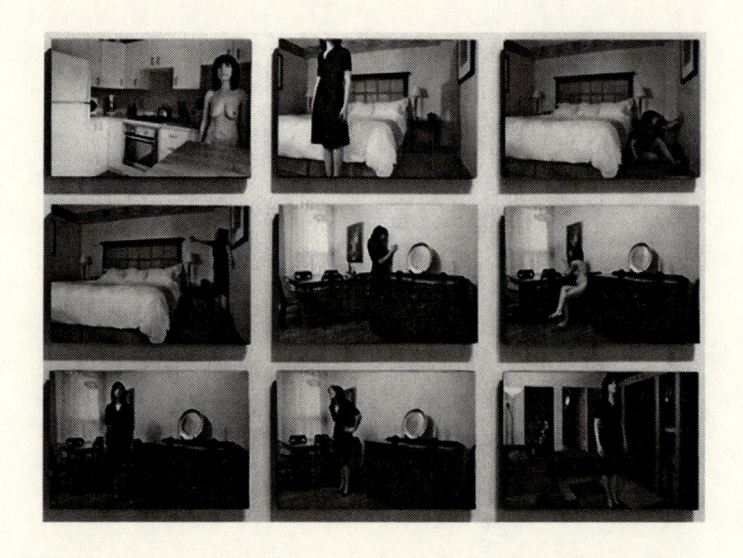

SF: It does, yes. In part it was a moment in which I fully permitted myself, without resistance, to follow the ideas my imagination foisted on me, and to let them supersede other ideas, such as that I had to present myself as attractive or even desirable, that I had to be the main subject of a self-portrait, that I was too much an amateur to attempt something on a larger scale. In retrospect, one thing I wish is it had been possible for me to shoot that piece with a male subject, or that I had liked the title rooms with person: it's very hard to move photographs of women outside the question of gender, particularly when domestic space is involved, and to me gender was never the subject of the work. Indeed, it's very much, in my own intent, about the mutuality of the shaping of architectural space and the shaping of selves; gender can enter into that, of course, but it happens outside of gender as well.

SQ: Yes, interiority is scripted "feminine." Deborah Bright talks about landscape as being a "preserve of American myths about Nature, Culture and Beauty," and it seems to me a good point historically, but why are women still so concerned with "self" and "interior?" I love Cindy Sherman's "Untitled Film Stills," and I love your series, and I'm not even sure that I think women need to shift their gaze "outside," but I do wonder how conscious we are of what we choose to focus on.

On the other hand, I don't think we've actually investigated these questions nearly enough, and it seems to me that your investigation takes an angle that I haven't seen – that architectural shaping of selves as you say. Can you say a little more about that? You photograph your own children, for example, but there too I get a sense of form rather than say, Sally Mann, who seems much more interested in documenting domesticity or perhaps we come back to emotion/confession.

SF: The feminist in me says that we as women are trained to see ourselves in an interior mode. I'm not very good at that (a close friend once told me I was actually born a post-operative transsexual, and that didn't feel wrong). I live domesticity, of course, like any other woman with children, but when I photograph it, I'm not thinking domesticity (except, occasionally, ironically or over deliberately). I'm currently working on a set of material with my children as subjects, and we've talked about how to construct the photographs so that they have the potential to not be about them as children. Photographs of men are not always about masculinity; I knock my head all the time against the idea of photographs of women being fundamentally about them as women etc. I don't want to have to photograph men in order to say something that isn't gender-specific. So I won't. Maybe eventually I'll be able to be seen that way.

SQ: Where do images such as "Door" fit in to your series work? It was one of the first photographs I recall seeing where you entered the scene. Does this represent a kind of bridge from *Rooms with Woman*, to *Eros*? The latter series represents a larger leap in terms of your specific interest in the body, but it seems to me that some of the images predate the Rooms series. I'm interested in this simply because I find the evolution of your work particularly intriguing, and some of my favourite works – seem somehow to refuse categorization. Of course, that unruliness intrigues.

SF: "Door" was, in the creation, partly an exploration of technique and partly an exercise in compulsion (I very rarely actually feel any need to photograph myself, but I did that day; that doesn't, however, mean that I actually consider this or its companion pieces to be self-portraits – I don't). In the end I found a release in them in accepting the outer limits of digital technology, though I've gone farther since then. There's a strong school of thought that digital noise is ugly; I think it's just new to us – there is no inherent reason for the preference of prominent film grain over the equivalent extremes of digital noise. Both are the technology showing themselves.

My erotica is less an interest in the body than an interest in the experience of erotica: I am interested in the line between erotica and pornography, in how we see and respond to erotic imagery. I would like to find ways of controlling that response that push the viewer from the comfortable into the uncomfortable, without drawing upon the standard tropes of S&M and the like fetishes, taboos, etc. There are more interesting lines than subject matter. In the meantime, I'm sure I'll end up showing work that's meant just to help me better understand how to light bare flesh. I'm a compulsive exhibitionist in the sense of not being very good at keeping photographs to myself.

<...>

SQ: Recently I saw a major exhibition of Jeff Wall's work at MoMA. I am always impressed by the amount of narrative he condenses in his work. One Wall image can seem like a series. And also, I think Wall is working with gesture in a similar way. Can you expand on this idea of the gesture and why it might be interesting to problematize our assumptions of reality?

SF: Gesture is one of the key methods we have of self-presentation, along with how we shape and dress our bodies gesture at the level of posture, of gait, as well as the more usual meaning of hand position and movement. To me it's one of many things I would like to bring to a conscious level. And this is where I think my work gets really old-fashioned. Because if we can be aware of something, we can take control of it; and if we can take control of our exteriority and alter it, then we can also alter our interiority — our selves — which are essentially the same thing. It's another tracing of the material world-culture-self triangle that's fascinated me for years. It's old-fashioned because, I like to think, art could maybe — just maybe — sometimes teach us to see something anew, and thus give us the potential for change.

<...>

SQ: I'm glad you brought up the addictive quality of instant feedback because I think it is stimulating, but as you say, it's also problematic in that it makes one want to perform, or shoot a particular subject. I think the question of how one strikes a balance between connecting with "an audience," and going deeply into oneself to direct the work is an important one. Can you tell me about that moment of understanding?

SF: It's nice to be liked, isn't it! I do find that I have to remind myself, often, that if I only seek to please an audience, I may miss my other goals. You can please an audience, even a large one, by giving them what they know they want. You can inspire an audience, or touch them deeply, move them, in the medieval sense of movere, by giving them what they didn't know they could want. Every once in a while you might get both, but I've learned that I get more satisfaction, personally, from the harder pleasure. Moving away from my established audience was a gesture to myself, both as a more concrete reminder that it wasn't that easy pleasure that mattered and as an act of faith in myself. If I could believe in the work enough not to test drive it, then I might be able to do even more.

‡ Thursday, July 19, 2007
Gentle, Juliana Spahr

Nature, what is nature? What is eco? What is eco-poetics? What is nature/eco-poetics? How does feminism fit into nature eco poetics? What would a Vendana Shiva-Donna Haraway hybrid look like? Tim Lilburn and Juliana Spahr? I can't help but wonder what, how, nature, or what we think of as nature, differs east, west, developed, undeveloped, with and without money, never mind north or south of our border, and more locally here, block by block, pulse by pulse, how we describe the leaf fluttering on our buffed shoulders as we raise our lattes and our poetic expectations. Obviously yes, it differs, it's the how that interests me, the exact quantity of more and less that depends on so many things: perspective, location, geography, the reading (and coffee drinking) tastes of the poet in question. Oh, didn't I mention poetry? Yes, what is nature poetry...

Gentle is not Spahr's most recent book, as I said, but it's the newest to me. Part catalogue, part prayer – a word that seems sorely out of place in this context but in fact that is why I want to use it. Taking back the idea of prayer, which is after all, everyone and anyone's business. As is nature. And now that "nature" is on everyone's mind, what are we thinking of? "We come into the world," Spahr begins, "We come into the world and there it is./ The sun is there." The sun is there, and already the rhythm is there, already the lines like small springs, or coils ready to move through the poem's machinations. "The brown of the river leading to the blue and the/brown of the ocean is there./ Salmon and eels are there moving between the brown/and the brown and the blue."

How does one see? A thing in movement, a pail attached to a tall spiky wood, snow, spring, light. What is the beetle carrying? How banana a slug? What temperature mist? How glisten the leaf tremble? Who tells us nature has a tone, a note, and that tone is reverent and that note "sincere?" Who says nature poetry has a certain straightforward language? Who says what is accessible? How is accessible described by a given group of individuals encountering poetry? I suspect the average reader is more prepared to have his or her mind blown than we know.

Reminiscent of Robertson's *The Weather* and Dionne Brand's *Thirsty* and *No Language is Neutral* and others – Lilburn, Joshua Beckman, the poems in *Gentle* go in waves, carry the reader, summer day, lake, lying on an air mattress, or better yet, rock, spring, head tilted up, out, look.

In *Vis-à-Vis,* Don McKay, who won the 2007 Griffin Prize for poetry, talks about the wild, that poetry comes from a place of wild seeing (or pre-language sensing?). Lilburn, as well, in both his essays and his poetry mkes this point. I think they recognize that seeing doesn't imply a singular way of viewing or of recording. Does nature insist on line breaks, for instance? How does form fit in nature poetry? "Our hearts took on the shape of the stream," Spahr writes; they "took on the shape of whirligigs swirling across the water," our "hearts took on many things." And poetry is, perhaps, how we carry that.

And maybe language poetry, whatever or however one might try to contain that, is a similar place of wild, a place of things not immediately named, a place of remaining open. And when the lyric impulse, that honest voice, that vulnerable stretto meshes with language, with intention, with procedure – then whatever side of the border or gender, or political spectrum the project may originate in, it knocks this reader out.

‡ Tuesday, August 14, 2007

Like fellow San Fransisco poet and artist Yedda Morrison, Elizabeth Treadwell works the seams between representations of nature, exposing the poem's underwires. Regarding Morrison's photographs:

> Fakery becomes a larger and more explicit element in later works in the series, such as Bioposy #4 (Underwires) and Bioposy #6 (Red Devil Green Beast), which reveal the plastic stems, coated wires, and punctured mounts usually hidden within arrangements of artificial flowers.
> – Georgia Strait

The impulse of blending natural and artificial is hardly news in either the poetry or art world. And yet, of course, it's still very much news. And more so the insistence on seeing the seams, where things meet, not just in terms of benign layers, but how human desire and its byproducts are factored in. "Conventional" poetry still clings to pristine representations of the natural world, resists the impulse to include the scruffy and toxic underbelly of the water's surface.

As Joshua Corey points out here in the procedings from Vancouver's AWP Conference, "there is barely any distance to travel between Wordsworth's 'The Daffodils' and virtually any poem of Mary Oliver's you would care to name." To be fair, I've heard Oliver say she never intended to be a nature poet, and certainly not an eco or experimental writer. Perhaps she simply wants to write a life of quiet observation – not carrying a weight of chronicling the unseen in what she is seeing, and with little reference to a wider body of reading or theory. Many poets do – and those that do, seem very concerned with those who don't. But never mind, and never mind that the "nature" in a Mary Oliver poem, though never stated, comes in the form of a national park or a groomed yard. Here is Corey again:

> Oliver's plain poetic speech, meant to serve as a marker of both accessibility and authenticity, represses the strangeness and vitality of language beyond its usefulness as a resource. Her language gestures at wildness, tries to terrify you like a lion at the end of a leash — but it is tame, and we never lose sight of the lion tamer's whip and chair.

Again, not news, and yet, yes...news. I've been thinking about this post for weeks, and there are more words in the recycling bin than here because it just isn't simple...none of this is.

Treadwell, like Spahr (and every Belladonna poet), seeks to reinvigorate language with new meaning. How in a world where everyone is expecting everyone else to be lying, can we see language as anything more than the glint of surface, a way to facilitate given financial transactions? (Yes, they've just hit the miners trapped underground in Utah. Someone is tunneling under Gaza. The U.S. is busy privatizing Iraq as CAConrad points out...). My mind just flipped over into Spahr's *This Connection of Everyone With Lungs*, which impacts with similar associative leaps:

> Here is today.
>
> Over eight million people marched on five continents against the mobilization.

and later:

> We talked on the phone about this glimmer.
>
> We read each other's reports.

> We said optimistic things.

Language attempting to grapple with the sheer quantity of modernity. The number of bodies that can pile up to try and say no, and yet are unheard, even as we tally, they are unheard... What do words mean in the face of this? "As I thought about this, life went on," Spahr says.

And Treadwell too with her disassociate junctures:

> a fair measure of helicopter trees, when mothers
> skirt is blinded in the photosun, and never linger.

Where Treadwell dismantles, Spahr begins to both detonate and reconstruct. Perhaps these impulses, not the new sincerity, nor the new/neo/retro formalism, is where poetry can be useful.

This post is far from complete...

One wonders why readers of a forum such as a blog meant to disperse ideas, thinking and influence, continually privilege one voice/blogger over another? And one wonders too where or what the future of poetry blogs might be if this is the case. Will they be subsumed under one banner or another as has been the case with the Poetry Foundation, which seems bent on reaching out to a slightly wider audience, at least in terms of its online presence, or those mega-bloggers who seem bent on having every item of poetry pass through their fingers? Or the linksters – those who scour google and provide us with poetry links, no digesting or commentary, just the links. Or perhaps it will all move to facebook?

‡ Saturday, November 03, 2007
Living utopia and disaster

Thank God for art, that's all I can say. So much art seems to me to be so much better at moving one, not to mention making one think, in new ways. The Alberta Biennale of Contemporary Art at the Walter Phillips Gallery at the Banff Centre makes it just a little easier to deal with the environmental anxiety roiling barely under the surface these days.

> For the 6th incarnation of the Alberta Biennial of Contemporary Art, curators Catherine Crowston and Sylvie Gilbert have undertaken an investigation of the dual themes of Utopia and Disaster within the context of Alberta and its relation to the world environment.

While I'm not quite sure yet what the context of Alberta is in its relation to world environmental devastation and while I would have wished for something that hit closer to home, I'm excited by the number of brilliant pieces. Highlights include Jennifer Bowe's luxurious blanket woven of text, Anu Guha-Thakurta's scraps of ephemera pinned daintily to a wall, shadows sturdy as pegs. Some of the work is very on point: Chris Flodberg's triptych of paintings of dogs tearing at food – above them a banquet laid out and behind that an urban world crumbling. Others are a little more slant: an empty room with a camera waiting to be interacted with, the only possible outcome a grayscale of self from Kay Burns. Jonathan Kaiser's installation is a room filled with the sound of rushing water, half a dozen empty fish tanks, holes stopped up, seaweed spilling through the roof, and a transom over the door showing water rising and rising... One of the most moving and powerful workds is Mary Kavanagh's installation of videos embedded in small holes (4x6) that show people frolicking on what first seems to be a beach but turns out to be the White Sands missile testing grounds. The works do, as the curators hope, illustrate the wild swings between depression – there's not a hope in hell for either the human race, or the planet – and optimism – we haven't even begun to imagine what innovation can mean!

‡ Monday, November 05, 2007
Sexism in poetry?

Big discussion over at Harriet, the *Poetry Foundation's* blog, regarding the numbers (real stats folks) in relation to women and publishing. Is this a shock to anyone? Really? I'm thankful to Juliana Spahr and Stephanie Young for doing this work. It's important work, thankless, and generally gets you nowhere. And great that the *Chicago Review* has published this, provided the graphics, and made the essays available on their website for those of you who don't subscribe.

For my part, I don't argue anymore – I just take up space.

‡ Tuesday, December 04, 2007
Blogging vs. journaling

Blogging has been an obsession of many, curtailed recently by the Facebook obsession in which communication is reduced to one-line updates framed in the language of the program... Even pre-Facebook, I was wondering what the impact of so much online "writing" would be on the art of keeping a diary, or a journal (let alone its impact on publishing). Particularly, as I suspect that for many, blogging has replaced the journal, and in some cases, publishing too.

Part of the appeal of reading the diaries of this or that person is the surprise of perspective. Although I am not naive enough to think that famous people don't think their diaries will be read, I do think that they are nonetheless, candid. The good ones in any case, the ones we want to read. How can it be otherwise? Who is interested in reading a journal in which the author isn't giving her opinions freely? Who is interested in reading a journal of repression? Delusion maybe, but repression?

On the other hand, the fact that we currently report on every moment of our lives, makes it seem quite impossible that at some point in the future, we will find those lives of interest. If we are currently publishing every thought, every response, every flickering mood, will there be anything left to say? Who will care to read the letters of our generation? Or, will it be the letters of those who have resisted the technologization of their craft that we turn to in wonder? There is a posse of Luddite nature poets banking on that...

As Louis Menand points out in the *New Yorker* recently, we read diaries so that we can see each other through someone else's eyes. In the following excerpt, Woolf's eyes:

> Pale, marmoreal Eliot was there last week, like a chapped

> office boy on a high stool, with a cold in his head, until he warms a little, which he did. We walked back along the Strand. "The critics say I am learned & cold" he said. "The truth is I am neither." As he said this, I think coldness at least must be a sore point with him. (February 16, 1921.)

Or

> Edith Sitwell has grown very fat, powders herself thickly, gilds her nails with silver paint, wears a turban & looks like an ivory elephant, like the Emperor Heliogabalus. I have never seen such a change. She is mature, majestical. She is monumental. Her fingers are crusted with white coral. She is altogether composed. (July 23, 1930)

Or

> Dr. Freud gave me a narcissus. Was sitting in a great library with little statues at a large scrupulously tidy shiny table. We like patients on chairs. A screwed up shrunk very old man: with a monkey's light eyes, paralysed spasmodic movements, inarticulate: but alert. (January 29, 1939)

What must very quickly become apparent is that not only are we seeing through the eyes of an amazing human being, we are seeing with great detail and insight, into another world. An extremely well crafted world, even at her casual best. Not only another time, but another class – for many of us – another aesthetic. We are also, as Menand suggests, seeing a writer at her peak, absolutely enjoying the exercising of her craft, her wit, her salty pen.

If we make our worlds, if there is in fact no other world apart from the one we create, then let us at least create worlds of depth and movement and stillness and nuance and sharp portraits, even if they are – as they can be with Woolf – scathing. As for Facebook, as I said earlier, I resist all attempts to be pooled into a unit that will ultimately be commodified. That Facebook didn't have all the annoying ad content of Myspace was one of the reasons I could finally succumb. Even the blogging format offends me with its limitations and prescriptions...but I have learned to live with that, as I've learned to live with MS Word, Gmail, iPhoto, and the many limitations of my daily ware.

Facebook on the other hand? I'm not sure.

Why does it take a wannabe corporation to create an online forum for a bunch of poets and writers who want to stay in touch? For a while it was blogs doing that – but does anyone read blogs anymore?

‡ Tuesday, December 11, 2007
Richard Serra, Time, Poetics

I originally posted this photograph along with a response to that Serra show at the Gagosian in 2006, and somehow, it's fitting to see Lisa Robertson here among the sculptures.

While the materials, and impulse couldn't be more different, the attention and weight of achievement, is not dissimilar. In some ways Robertson's *The Weather* is another kind of displacement, à la Edward Burtynsky and Kim Huyhn, displacement as a means of making aspects of modernity explicit, a twist we are clearly in need of, given contemporary art's preoccupation. The project begins, in some way, with a question of perspective. Valazquez's *Las Meninas* was apparently an epiphany for Serra. The painting, he says, "opened up countless contradictory interpretations, none of which answered the questions posted by its perspective..." but ultimately it seems to be about breaking the frame and losing the "I."

Oddly enough, Vancouver artist, Jeff Wall, another Hound favourite, also claims *Las Meninas* as an essential moment. And like Serra, Wall deals in scale, in making monumental the materials of the world. Not as explicit as someone like Burtynsky, perhaps, but nonetheless, dealing with the conditions and by-products of modernity and capitalism. What makes these particular projects worthy of note? Well, scale, yes, and the degree to which the idea is investigated. Not merely hinted at, not one shot at getting it right; the interrogations of these artists gather over time.

I've been coveting Richard Serra's *A Matter of Time*, a gorgeous book from Guggenheim Bilbao that covers much of his early work. The surprise of perspective, the harsh contrast of lines of the early embedded work, to the grand, prow-like furls of the latter. Looking at sculpture from Serra, one gets a sense of dense calm. A thud of consciousness. Time flowing and immovable simultaneously. Deep calm. It's interesting that minimalism can achieve this in terms of scale...not sure what that means. Minimalism as a modernist echo.

Serra acknowledges a Zen influence, catching that wave of "everything connected," which is much more believable once one comes to terms with his scale. At first I, like many people I've spoken to, was offended by the grand gesture. It seemed a kind of gross over-compensation ...extremely masculinist and perhaps even wasteful. I have since changed my mind. This is what comes of being an art lover without art training — context sometimes arrives after the fact.

I'm intrigued by the friendship of Richard Serra and Robert Smithson too. In *A Matter of Time*, Serra states that his conversations with Smithson were never replicated. But one doesn't have to be alive to be in conversation. The work continues to grow, it seems to me. Good work in any case. Of his own process, Serra notes "at a certain point it was necessary for me to construct a language based on a system that would establish a series of conditions to enable me to work in an unanticipated manner and provoke the unexpected." The list became (and here I am condensing) as follows:

> to roll, to crease, to fold, to store, to bend, to shorten, to twist, to dapple, to crumple, to shave, to tear, to chip, to spit, to cut, to sever, to drop, to remove, to simplify, to differ, to dissarrange, to open, to mix, to splash, to knot... to hang, to collect — of tension, of gravity, of nature, of grouping, of layering, of felting — to grasp, to tighten...

and so on."The verb list," he suggests, "established a logic whereby the process that constituted a sculpture remains transparent..."

Of course what I wonder is where this energy appears in poetry. Is there a corresponding modernist sculptural poetic? And in terms of a lyric aesthetic, I'm still not convinced that the "I" in question, the "I" that needs to be gotten rid of, actually goes anywhere. Perhaps what is gotten rid of is a simplistic "I" the I that is only one of the pillars of the "w" in "We."

‡ Thursday, February 07, 2008
Jasper Johns

What a curious event, the art opening. What a melange of people and attire and desire. Though at least at an opening of an icon like Jasper Johns they use stemware. The wine, though white, was good. And they had gorgeous, lithe young men circulating with silver trays to disperse the stemware, which they refilled and refilled, and offered sparkling water too.

That was civilized.

But what an odd assortment of people. A few of the regular Chelsea sort: the thousand dollar shoes, the Vuitton bags, the Chanel clutch, the many layered hair, the outstanding pink ruffle coat, the fur, the linen, the blue tinted glasses, the yellow tinted glasses, the Burberry, the camel hair, the silky hair, the young with art bags in tow, the stranger in a Red Sox cap (treachery!) with odd collections of celebrity photos flipped here and there to what end one can't imagine... The latter dipping into the other end of the spectrum of attendee: the kind with many bags – some of which seemed to have contained cats at one point or another so clawed they were from the inside out, the kind, in short, who have no more use for art than they do lobster forks. Not that the Hound has any use for lobster forks either, but she is more selective in her baggage.

But the art. Lets not forget the art. There was Johns in the lovely, spacious Matthew Marks, his trademark greys the numbers, the combination of lines and circles, the playful, the abstract, in ink, charcoal, graphite pencil, watercolour, acrylic, pastel...the combination of said things on paper. The whimsy, the figures that often remind of bpNichol and to some extent bill bisset. This was the last stop in a long day of art.

Can we say that we were moved by Johns? Impressed by the weight of a career that has had such an impact on abstract art? A simultaneous show at the Met after all? It isn't fair, but I wanted to be in a room full of those early greys...

‡ Sunday, February 17, 2008
*We are what we read and think,
where we read and think*

She knows that where she reads and writes affects how and what she produces as much as what she reads and thinks. Wondering what she would produce if she had access to the new Seattle Public Library designed by Rem Koolhaas on a daily basis.

Would she cool? Would she simmer? Would she leap? Would the text be stark, the lines clean, conceptual, without stray words or emotion? Would she escalate? Would she levitate? Would she fire new neurons? Would she make new connections? New ways of seeing? Would the colours be bold? Well chosen and luminous? Would she gravitate toward modernist texts? (More than she already does that is...) Would she suddenly see beyond post-post modern? Would her thinking leap over form entirely, or would it be tripped up by it? Made aware of it? Of course location and design influence thinking. How can they not? And what we read affects what we write...

‡ Thursday, February 21, 2008
So much talk between women

Women and poetry. They just never stop talking about it. Crowding up the comments boxes all over the Internet. Tossing off opinions everywhere. Telling everyone else they're wrong. Got it backward. Forgot the most important poet ever. Don't know squat about this school or that. Mastheads overflowing with women. Women blogging about poetry and art. Women with opinions out there taking up space. Defining whole movements. Women with posses tagging them daily, hourly, reassuring little pats on their backs... Women reviewing and asserting grand theories, ways of organizing the canons. No wonder all the men are busy talking quietly amongst themselves...they can't get a word in.

‡ Tuesday, April 08, 2008
Autoportraits: Conversation with Stacy Szymaszek

LH: I've been focusing on the energy of the body moving through the city, but that's looking out I realize, and we're supposed to be thinking about self-portraits! Did you see the recent *New Yorker* piece on Sabrina Harman's self-portraits at Abu Ghraib? It's disturbing and far from your project, but it does speak to our cultural obsession with the self-portrait and how entrenched we are in it as a practice. I think your portraits break out of this surface obsession in their dense emotional reality. They allow for complex, unexplained, unfiltered emotion, something that it seems to me contemporary poetry has trouble with…was this something you were aware of?

SS: It is disturbing, not only in her obsession to photograph injury (and not to document any wrong doing) but then she needed to be in the photograph, smiling, thumbs up, like a tourist. A severe and creepy disconnect.

I wasn't consciously thinking about using self-portraiture to allow for emotion or to compensate for lack of it, but I'm not surprised you find it there. I think in all of my work, I'm going for emotional impact and not in a cheap way. I actually think it's a challenge to figure out what is moving beyond the surface level. In poetry I find it more in the way the work moves, the soundscape of it more than in anything posited as "emotional" – a poet who knows her material, which is language, is capable of getting to me. As a self-portraitist and in general, someone who is fascinated by people's "facades," I can look at 50 shots of my face and recognize the one that conveys complexity.

That series of photos in the OMG book are really photos of me proposing another gender story. The bathroom, all those faucets and mirrors, is such a powerful site for transformation, playing with identity. It's where we go to ready ourselves for the world, my favourite place to take pictures. So the intensity is there in my desire to be both more than what I am and less than what I am. A restlessness but also with a sense of freedom through posturing so people can see what I need them to see of me in that moment.

LH: We've talked about photography before, and I know you have an ongoing project of self-portraiture (and now a chapbook). How did your interest in photography/self portraiture get started? Is there something liberating about a poet looking out? And what happens when the looking out is then refracted back?

SS: I only started taking pictures in 2006. Before that time I didn't have the Internet at home or a cell phone or a digital camera. When I moved to NY I was fascinated by how these technologies facilitated community and interaction while at the same time complicated it. So I got a camera, and I was smitten – with my girlfriend, the camera, my friends, my social life, the areas of the city I dwelled in – so a lot of it came out of documentary impulse and an erotic one. My interest in self-portraiture, or more aptly in literature, persona, is evident in my poetry as far back as *Mutual Aid* where I'm kind of positing myself as geologist anarchist Kropotkin, then James, then I cast myself as Pasolini, and in *Hyperglossia* I manifest as Eustace.

It was a natural extension for me to turn the camera on myself, to play with digital depiction of my body. I really love Mapplethorpe's "Autoportrait" Polaroids so the OMG title is in homage to him.

You know that I participated in a group where the challenge was to take a self-portrait everyday for a year. I only got to about 160. I just don't have as much energy for any photography at the moment, and I feel like it's time for me to actually learn something about how to use my nice camera before I proceed. Throughout the daily self-po process I really got into controlling my image, using the fact that I'm fairly photogenic, and don't have a poker face, to make provocative pictures. I just remembered this story. When I was a freshman in college, I was interested in a guy, and I called his room and started a conversation with him. He asked me to point my picture out in the directory, so I did, and he was like, oh sweeeet, and came right over. I opened the door and his face dropped and he walked away. Fantasy, right? It's really a funny kind of power. He thought he was going to get laid and a wide-eyed "overweight" lesbian opens the door. I wasn't the one who was surprised.

128

I don't think I feel liberated by taking pictures, but it is a nice contrast to thinking about language (though image making is just as mysterious), and as I am a pretty desk-bound writer, I like that the camera gets me moving around, engaging with my environment differently.

‡ Thursday, April 24, 2008
The shark is always attracted by a bit of bloodletting

Ah, biography. There are those who offer painstaking illumination of their subject, those who fall into the pit of awe, the quick sand of over-reverence, and there are those, such as Janet Malcolm, who like to give their subjects a good lashing. This seems to give the author much pleasure, and well, perhaps her readers too? Having read the excerpts published over the years in the *New Yorker*, I wasn't expecting much from the book, but how could I resist a biography of Stein? She and Toklas are compelling, not only because of the books, the documentation of a modernist moment, the literary influence, and so on, but because of their various identities and the fact that they were able to live them out so fully. Particularly given when and where they lived them out.

Not surprisingly, Janet Malcolm's project rests on the question of how Stein and Toklas managed to survive the Second World War in Nazi-occupied France. Compelling, yes. And one wonders, one does want more information. And we are given some information in the form of Bernard Faÿ – a homosexual, a Catholic and a collaborator. Is this altogether surprising? Stein was conflicted politically, did not seem to want to bother with politics in a direct way, and there is more than one slant reference to unseemly connections in her own writing. One assumes that there were forces at work.

The facts are glaring, and one must wrestle with them, but Malcolm offers little insight into the episode because, quite frankly, there isn't much to illustrate. What is curious to me is the narrative of obliviousness that she crafts for Stein – a strand rooted in the by-now clichéd crtique of Stein's ego (we know all that...), her status as last born child, a person with a sense of things "always working out for herself" and then doing so. (In a way, Stein is a perfectly modern American subject isn't she? Just imagine help and abundance and it will arrive...). It would be interesting to imagine the making of that ego and the implications of it, the uses of it in terms of the risk of her multiple and complex identities.

The chapter on *Making of Americans* reads like a piece from *Vanity Fair* circa 1986 and might have been written by someone like Dominick Dunne (though in fairness there were moments when I thought of Lytton Strachey's *Imminent Victorians* too). In fact, I would have enjoyed it in the context of *Vanity Fair,* I'm sure, though I might have expected a little more bite, more stylish detailing, a body, some blood... On the other hand, kudos to Malcolm for actually making it through the novel, twice (I admit to not finishing it myself) and for her reading of the actual text, which I wish there had been more of. Frustratingly, Malcolm opts for a simple conclusion that Stein simply "can't invent" "can't write fiction," and while I agree that the text is a kind of self-discussion, a working out of the project, I think there is much more to say about her process in creating what is a very useful failure of a novel.

In fact, rather than going on about Stein's failure as a novelist, it would have been productive to think about the impossible nature of her undertaking, which after all, isn't news. Perhaps someone else will take up that project – other than Ulla Dydo who is both painted for the major Stein scholar she is, and again, made into a *Vanity Fair* character (as are the other Stein scholars).

There is a sense of playfulness (claws out, not in) in the text, as the *New York Times* points out, and it does achieve Malcolm's goals, which are clarity and engagement (goals that make her a frustrating choice for writing about Stein). In short, it's too bad that the playfulness wasn't used in the illumination of her subject or her subject's text, rather than the biographer herself. But then, people will likely not read this for Stein but for Malcolm's signature style, which leads one to wonder whether the book has any use as a means of furthering interest in Stein in the general, biography consuming public, that is outside of the avant-garde?

Over at *The Guardian* they had a much more sober, insightful review, which rightly points out Malcolm's overly moralizing tone, the finger pointing from one Jewish intellectual to another. Malcolm offers up a few self-revelations, which mirror in some ways, the most vicious attacks on Stein. I leave you with the last paragraph:

> This self-denying attitude (Toklas later and ostentatiously became a Roman Catholic) is really the driving force of *Two Lives*. So it is puzzling that Malcolm, who

is a present narrator throughout her own text, never mentions her own European Jewish heritage. While the Misses Stein and Toklas camped out in eastern France, baby Janet was being hurried from Prague to the safety of East Coast America. One is left unsure whether her reticence on this point is a sign of exquisite and deliberate judgment, or a highly significant oversight. One thing is certain: if she found such an odd loose end in one of her subject's lives, she'd seize it like a terrier and never let go.

And yes, there is a terrier like quality to Malcolm who enjoys her snipes, and enjoys working the bottom out from under a subject. The unearthing of the Leon Katz strand in *Making of Americans* was certainly worthwhile. Do we dare hope for this elusive information pertaining to the missing documents and the early stages of the writing of that novel? By the sounds of things, no. But now we might have some energetic minds who can get at the work and, as Ulla Dydo points out via Malcolm, create a bridge to the novel and unlock some of its secrets for would-be scholars.

Perhaps the most useful review comes from Terry Castle in the *London Review of Books*, who glories in Malcolm's abrasive bitchiness while sketching out both strengths and weaknesses of her text. My irritation has subsided somewhat, and I can see the fun in Malcolm's bite for example, ending a chapter with the line "we may assume that pussy's way would not have been her own." But I remain troubled by the insistence on painting Stein as a failed fiction writer, and I'm not sure what, aside from a kind of oblique titillation, Malcolm wanted to get at in the last section with the following quote from Hemingway: "She used to talk to me about homosexuality and how it was fine in and for women and no good in men and I used to listen and learn and I always wanted to fuck her and she knew it."

It is perhaps unfair to want a biographer to like her subject, and perhaps, even unwise. Rather one wants a range of responses and certainly more neutrality. But if one is going to take up the trope of the scathing and insouciant biographer, one might want to have something to say not only about one's subject, but about one's relationship to it, something to back up the penchant for the whip of a good quip, for the flaying of the unfortunate object who has managed to catch her eye. It isn't that I was looking for a love affair with Stein, it's that I was looking for some genuine insight.

‡ Thursday, July 10, 2008
Vanessa Place

I first heard of Vanessa Place and Les Figues in a cab going from JFK to midtown. I was with fellow poet Christan Bök who had much to say about Place, the press, and the upcoming n/oulipo publication (a compendium of the noulipo conference). Then I saw the novel and was smitten.

Relative newcomer Vanessa Place, a criminal appellate attorney and co-founder of the magnificent Les Figues Press, offers a 50,000 word, one-sentence novel set in World War I, and often right in the trenches of it. Circumnavigating, diverging, listing, relishing in the feast of language on so many levels...it comes out, as Stein says, and after a while it doesn't have to come out ugly. This is the price paid for all the experimenting...our "crisis jubilee"....

Dies: A Sentence is a thing of beauty right from the beginning:

> The maw that rends without tearing, the maggoty claw that serves you, what, my baby buttercup, prunes stewed softly in their own juices or a good slap in the face, there's no accounting for history in any event, even such a one as this one, O, we're knee-deep in this one, you and me, we're practically puppets, making all sorts of fingers dance above us, what do you say, shall we give it another whirl, we can go naked, I suppose, there's nothing to stop us and everything points in that direction, do you think there will be much music later and of what variety, we've that, at least, now that there's nothing left, though there's plenty of pieces to be gathered by the wool-coated orphans and their musty mums, they'll put us in warm wicker baskets, cover us with a cozy blanket of snow, and carry us home...

Difficult to excerpt, but my experience with it so far is really one of waves, small, very distinct movements that blend one into the other. And the language! Check this out:

> there was sausage in my veins and roast pork beneath my feet, what's worst you say, you callous bastard, how can you squat there armlessly stirring a pot of camp stew and feign sudden irony, it'll get you nowhere, you know, that bit of levity one wears like a rubber nose in the face of cold terror, such weak crooked lenitive proves a man's uncrutch...

Not since *The Waves* have I been compelled to read an experimental novel through. Not just to appreciate the concept but to actually read it through...and I am still reading and thinking about what makes conceptual fiction work. And why does this one seems to work so well? I've made it through to the end, but only because I had to for the sake of discussion. I'm going through again, and it's a slow, sensual pleasure and a much deserved break from various essays on the boil. Vanessa Place agreed to talk to me via email. Due to time constraints our conversation has taken place over weeks, and it isn't finished either. I offer you round one.

LH: Vanessa, from what I can gather, *Dies* is your first published novel, but surely you have written fiction before that?

VP: This suggests *Dies* is fiction, which suggests interesting issues of form and institutional critique. The shortish answer is I had been working on a large project *(La Medusa)* and wrote *Dies* between drafts. I spent about 10 years writing *Medusa*; the first draft of *Dies* was written in about three months sometime around year four. I then put *Dies* away, and returned to the bigger monster. I did write a few odds and ends along the way, pieces published as everything from experimental nonfiction to straight poetry, but no sustained work. After finishing my final draft of *Medusa*, I took *Dies* out and polished it for Les Figues. Happily, Fiction Collective 2 is publishing *Medusa* this August.

LH: I should have said "prose" rather than fiction. Is your resistance one of genre, or form?

VP: I have no resistance to form, which would be like having a resistance to red clay, or lead white. Genre's the thing, foolish thing, oddly stubborn. The most avant-seeming people ask you straight-faced if you are a poet or a fiction writer. I find yes is a very good answer. It reassures the questioner, without solving the question. Rather like answering whether someone is guilty or innocent.

LH: Where did the idea for *Dies* come from? Was it an idea that morphed, or a project that you proposed and then fulfilled?

VP: *Dies* was contrapuntal. As noted, I had been working on a very big project composed of very many fragments for a very long time, and wanted a palate-cleanser. The plate-spinning of the larger work immediately suggested its opposite: a single form that falls constantly, though incompletely, apart. The sentence is the basic formal unit of prose, counted as the container of thought. Shortly thereafter, I saw a photograph of a WWI soldier crossing a field who had gotten a leg snagged in some wire, and wondered what it would be like to be suspended in that wait, anticipating the bullet or blast that you cannot escape but can only attempt to negotiate. Death marks, or punctuates, the basic formal unit of human existence; death is the basic human sentence. The formal question becomes how to kill the sentence, how to grope pathetically towards "Death, once dead there's no more dying then."

LH: The torn leg is one of the tropes that leads us through the text. It's a powerful image, and speaks to the obvious disconnect of war and carnage, but also to our investment in compartmentalization I think. Was that something you were thinking about?

VP: Fragments, I suppose, are always on the mind. They can be a bit of a cheat as they too easily serve as synecdoche, but are not a cheat in that they also incant the missing, playing the positive role of negative space. Compartmentalization is a gorgeous device for feigning wholeness, just as warrens create the illusion of connection and at least the potential for movement. Stew is good for food.

LH: "Death marks, or punctuates, the basic formal unit of human existence; death is the basic human sentence..." This is intriguing, and certainly forces one to think of text literally as body. I'm thinking too of Stein's bumpy ride through the first world war, which one feels here. As one feels the resistance to closure. A resistance that becomes emblematic of a desire to live. Which leads me to ask, is this found text?

VP: That's a wonderful question; I wish it were, or I wish I'd thought of incorporating found elements within its folds. But aside from the Hugh MacDiarmid poem near the beginning of the book, it's all my creation. That makes me slavish to that same desire, I think.

LH: I am astounded at the deft way you shift in and out of consciousness. I'm working through the novel and I keep being distracted by my desire to pinpoint transitions. They are so seamless. How did you do that?

VP: I like to listen while I'm talking.

LH: As you know I'm a big fan of Beckett. Could he have been a figure in *Dies?*

VP: He could have been its wet nurse.

Friday, August 01, 2008
A Pair of Scissors, a bit of snipe

The Capilano Review has a special issue on Sharon Thesen worth checking out, and in conjunction with that I offer a little morsel I've been pondering what to do with for some time now. Whether in fact I should make it public. It speaks less about Thesen than to a kind of cultural and intellectual rift between a certain strand of poet one encounters, not only in New York, though I encountered quite a number there, and of a certain intensity. In any case, that's where this tale begins, in a book store in New York – The Strand to be exact – where I was perusing one day and I came across a copy of Thesen's *A Pair of Scissors*. I already had the book, but given the contents felt compelled to buy again and did for $6. It came, as many books of Canadian poetry do in used bookstores in New York, with the press release tucked neatly inside, the spine barely cracked. This one however, had actually been read, and it came with marginalia and correspondence from a Canadian literary journal regarding a review of this and other books. The New York reviewer, who shall remain nameless here, is apparently a member of Mensa, a fan of Mae West, and reviewer of poetry – Brenda Shaughnessy, for example – and in the *American Book Review*. I haven't seen any review by her of *A Pair of Scissors*, so perhaps none was ever published. However, I have some sense of what she might have wrote, assuming the copious notes in the margins belong to the addressee in the polite letter from the Canadian literary journal, which will also remain nameless.

There is, from the outset, some irritation with Thesen. In "The Forests of the Taiga," a reference to a reclusive woodland caribou is apparently worth noting, and on the same page, "sustainable development" is underlined with "mocking tone" written next to it. This followed by the line "nobody speaks for the whole system" and its companion comment: "yes⁄nobody⁄not even Sharon Thesen." By the next page the would⁄be reviewer notes "journalistic prose, like a notebook entry," and later she recognizes "irony" in a line or two. "Good poem," she notes, though "language and expressions are uneven," revealing that particular kind of new formalist bias against the casual, the unpolished, the unseemly being referenced in a poem. Not the place for such things. I've heard this particular brand of poet say, one wants the appropriate hint of the real.

"The Bikers at Lund, July Long Weekend," is "interesting" in its "observations and metaphors," and "Victoria Day Weekend, Silverton," is outed for being "pretend" haiku featuring "mundane life," a fact highlighted several times throughout, in terse letters. "Some Thesen poems make you shrug and say 'so what?'" our reviewer notes. "Lattes!" She feels compelled to note on another. Good lord, not lattes! And on another "Can't get all the Canadian references!!!" Much, much irritation by now. Straining to find connections to American poets. By the time we get to "Moon over Starbucks" the reviewer notes "References to popular culture offend me." By page 52, the entries are sparse, but in the bottom left corner next to the closing couplet in a sonnetish form, "And keep the woods besides.⁄The woods so beautiful and relaxed," one hopeful note: "Frost⁄echo?"

By page 55, she's about to give up: "Cheapens her poems with references to objects, brands, makes it like an ad..." The last word underlined for emphasis. But by now it's clear she is not a fan of Thesen: "too self-referential." Another offending aspect to poetry for this Strand of poet. One must be self-referential but not obviously, not ironically; it has to be an "ah" kind of self-referentiality. And who are all these poets? Underlined, double-underlined? Roy who? Newlove who? (One can reference poets, but they should be known poets!) The very, very occasional "good" is written tentatively next to a line, but mostly this reviewer is pissed off: "self-important pouffe," she concludes after a poem about the BC Book Prizes.

Here is the poem "Magpie":

> park on the street to pick up
> a chick-pea samosa, a *New Yorker*
>
> on the way home from work teaching –
> these bloodlettings we call work, just
> open a vein I y'am what I y'am a human
> aquifer

Our reviewer offers the following comment written above:

> self referential moaning
> writing is easy, just open a vein.
> when Sharon is moaning,
> she's maudlin.

Here an attempt to scan, here an attempt to count lines: "every now and then a rhyme as easy as a drive-by..." "Irritating tic of using commas and then not using commas...", "so pale next to DHL." "Good but too long" and finally "Ugh." Now and then underlines, double underlines (not sure what to make of those). On one page "the king needs a jester," and on another a big star with the following underlined so forcefully it seems to serrate the lines from the page:

> I mean, I don't want to bore the reader
> the way I've been bored, drained
> by ugly verbs, spilled into a toxic lake

What to make of it? Perhaps that's why I've carried it around. A kind of testament to an unwillingness to connect. A lack of appreciation for the art of self-deprecation one poet commented – and that's something I have witnessed much over the years. A lack of willingness to be present. Ever wonder why so much popular American poetry seems like it was written in the 19th century? Or is completely without reference to contemporary times? As you can see, this is something heavily policed in many journals – no modern references! None! How often does one find any political content in a poem in *The New Yorker*? Otherwise yes, but in a poem? Or how many Canadian place names? There's a reason why the local gets erased: it isn't the proper kind of local. At least for poetry.

In any case, as with most reviews, the notes say more about the would-be reviewer than about the poet's work. And to be fair they are notes. But they are notes toward a review. And what do our reading notes say about us? About the way we read? And what do our reviews say about us and the way we read? What tone do they take? What kind of generosity, intellectual curiosity, do they show of us? Do we enter into a text ready to make a grand defense of our own poetic, or are we really trying to appreciate the poet's world? Are we able to recognize another poet's operating system? What is revealed here is the utter inability to let go of one's own aesthetic, to read a poem that might not reflect what one already knows, or what one thinks poetry should be.

‡ Saturday, August 09, 2008
Make the world your salon

This goes out to the women who read *Lemon Hound* and other blogs. Those who don't comment, don't enter into public discourse. What would it be like to make the world your salon? To be as comfortable with one's opinion at a conference table, or weblog, or site otherwise filled with experts (all men, of course, with endless commentary designed to undermine your place at said table) as one is sitting across from friends in one's living room, a cup of tea and endless streams of commentary about everything from the design of the cup in hand to the possibilities of poetry as a political tool?

Looking at the media surfaces, the illuminations on the net and elsewhere, I tire of seeing women commenting on commentary, or the style sections of newspapers, as adornment, as fluff. On my own blog, a new list is building – that of the she-blog or other-blog. The voices outside the dominant streams of things. May it build. May it bite. What if Susan Sontag had blogged? What if Gertrude Stein or Mina Loy had blogged?

Make the world your salon.

‡ Sunday, October 26, 2008
Margaret Christakos notes toward an essay on

Christakos is a great reader of her work in terms of both her presentation of it performatively and in her discussion of it. Those up for poetry at 12:30 on a Monday and who managed to make it to the Simon deBeauvoir Institute were treated to a good hour of text, from both from *Sooner* and *What Stirs*, Christakos new book. *What Stirs* traces the notion of the "latch" both literally and figuratively as a sense of connection between mother and child, between reader and text, self and other, subject and referent, door and lock, and so on.

Christakos describes her own work as employing strategic word pairings harvested from the Internet and elsewhere to construct "forceful collages." The indeterminate narrator undoes, or troubles lyric expectations. The latter isn't perhaps news anymore (Hejinian, Howe, Moure, Robertson, Zolf, Riley, and so on), nor are Christakos methods of troubling lyric, but what she does with all of that certainly is original and effective. Thematically *What Stirs* operates as an exploration of the word "latch" and its many implications, most importantly the notion of entitlement and comfort. Grace Jones comes to mind here, her strangely haunting disco hit from the early 1980s in terms of our endless desire for comfort and capacity for entitlement. What if what we have is enough, Christakos asks. What if we are sated? Why are our fists still out for more?

One of the powerful forces at work in Christakos is the complicated representation of motherhood and domesticity. I talked about this in my essay on Canadian poetry for the *Gulf Coast Review*, but I say again, Christakos is the most inventive "domestic" poet I've ever encountered (other than perhaps Elizabeth Treadwell). Here, we see a poet/mother figure who traces desire textually/linguistically and literally through her texts, such as "News & Now," "Mumsy," and "Used":

> Be a letdown Always match Cleverly
> match the gaunt Be up up
> vain All the cleverly the punk
> bowtie with some nice elbows Zesty
>
> Almost gaunt.

The desiring mother with her nursery rhymes and status as President of the Frank Sinatra fan club serve as markers here, the text using the tropes of mother/child expectations: the repetitions that soothe and the differences that surprise and offer pleasure. Throughout the text, Christakos returns to latch, turning and turning the word on its head, so that we see the maternal subject negotiating her desire to resist the suction of the "latch" through costuming in poems such as "My Attache Case," for example, the usual shopping tropes in "Visual Splendour Coupons," and "Lost ('Immortal')." There is a lot of fun in this text. Very subversive fun. "Turret Door," had me laughing out loud:

> She lifted the hyphen dash and entered the turret door,
> while the lady and I waited below.
> He'll dash on fine initially, then he pulls off and pops
> himself back on with a shallow dash.
> The pink one has a hyphen dash for the lid and would
> look real cute on a chain.
> So they think because there is a hyphen dash you push

under a flange a bear could not watch you once and figure the whole thing out.
I will have to come up with some sort of hyphen dash.
I admit that I am an addict.
Dash hooking is my life.

The latch becomes what we click down, attempt to hold in place, rely on, undo and do. Finally, we see the very structures of language, letters latching one to the other, piercing and clicking our own tongues.

‡ Tuesday, October 07, 2008
The text is the text is the text or nothing is easier than making fun of Gertrude Stein

A sharp reminder of both of these facts at the Colloque International on Gertrude Stein at Université du Québec à Montréal last week. Marjorie Perloff gave a very good, old-fashioned close reading of Stein's portrait of Christian Berard. This reading, it seems, was in response to the recent Poem Talk installment out of the University of Pensylvania and the Kelly Writers House in which Jerome Rothenberg, Bob Perelman and Lee Ann Brown discuss the poem in question. The Poem Talk episode is called "A Portrait, But of Who?" Does it matter if this is a portrait of Berard and not Picasso, the panelists wonder? And, no, the panelists seem to agree, it doesn't. The portrait, panelists suggest, is indicative of Stein's larger project in the portraits, a sweeping statement that conflates each portrait. Which means what? That it's all a wash? That one thing can be another?

The text, Perloff reminds us, should be the primary site of our thinking and investigating, not the existing criticism or biography. I'm sure it's a matter of time before Perloff publishes the essay, at which point I urge you to take a closer look. I'm tempted to recount the nuances of her reading here, but suffice to say there is clear evidence of the specificity of the portrait.

Other excellent presentations included Joan Retallack's "Language and Pleasure. Stein, Stein, Stein, Stein, Stein," which was itself a pleasure. What struck me in her presentation was simply the relief of hearing someone enjoy what they were reading and engaging with. Not trying to trump Stein (as other participants did) but engaging with the text. "If you enjoy it, you understand it," Stein said. I'm not convinced that it's that simple, but for a minute, it's refreshing. There is something antagonistic about insistence that Retallack seemed to be saying gets at the "irrational, abject other within us..." that made good sense.

Barbara Cole, from SUNY Buffalo, gave a talk on Stein criticism, pointing out the overly familiar and bodily attacks used in language of reviewers. She started out with an anecdote about Jerry Seinfeld talking to Merv Griffin and Griffin interjecting a Steinian line that Seinfeld doesn't get, tries to fold into his joke, etc. Tried to find that one on youtube because it sounds too good to be true.

Lianne Moyes offered a reading of Gail Scott's *My Paris*, illuminating the use of French, and outlining some differences between Scott's Paris and Stein's Paris, while tracing influences and tensions in Scott's novel – more precisely, compositional strategies versus description. How much universilizing and erasure happens around Stein's commas? And what of Scott's use of the comma to include translation? I'm looking forward to the paper, and wanting to reread *My Paris* with this in mind.

Unfortunately, my French isn't good enough to report on the papers given by the French academics, but what I understood of Jean-Francois Chassay's "Euphemisme et politique: Stein et la bombe atomique," was brilliant. Made me want to do a reading of it here myself. Indeed, how can we think about the atomic bomb? "If I were a general I would never lose a battle, I would only mislay it..."

> Journalist: Why don't you write the way you talk?
> Stein: Why don't you read the way I write?

Friday, December 12, 2008
Virginia Woolf reads K. Silem Mohammad

"Formalism Doesn't Kill People"
A curious poem this morning. You will note the title above from a poet I have never met. Strange tensions from the beginning. I am assuming, given the tone of the poem, that the poem in question isn't what the poet thinks of as "formalism." I'm thinking too that Eliot might signify formalism – Eliot, Yeats, Byron and down. Though what might formalism mean now? And please, tell me poets aren't writing the same as the old poets? What would be the point in that? Though with all of these many poets zinging lines toward each other in the air, with a click, what does being a poet even mean?

But back to the poem, which suggests, if I'm reading my irony correctly, that formalism is the opposite of this poem. This poem starts with a series of observations. Small ball bearings that go forward and backward:

> a brave vastness (faith)
> dovetails with concerns
> of what music is

A poem like a necklace, gathering momentum, about nothing, it might seem. Tiny snapshots calling out to each other. A world I have no idea how to enter. A scrambled world of anachronism and quotation marks. Tonal. Exemplary. But I like the "brave vastness" contrasted with "faith," clearly lacking and mocking. I like dovetailings in with concerns and music – a natural pairing? What a strange meshing together of words without, it seems, attention to meaning:

> thinking being analogous
> to "breakthroughs"
> turns them into formalist armatures
>
> abstract or optical effects bend words
> to painting's non-retrospective
> melting plaid center

It does make one reconsider each word. "Armature," for example, a word that has morphed from meaning "armour," or "arms," from the Latin armatura, to suggest a motor, or coils in a motor, how they are structured one assumes, to create energy. So the poem speaks to the aspects of formalism, as is suggested here, and relies on structure to create coherence. The "abstract or optical effects" create these non-retrospective melting plaid centres. The poet does seem to shake out these words and render them fresh, crisp, more themselves, if that is possible. What is a plaid centre? An intersection? A meeting place? Something non-retrospective must be non-representative, the new formation playing on the many layers of realism and romanticism laden with the word "representation." As I once said of Donne, this poet "leaps into poetry the shortest way." This poet offers a new kind of poetry: punctuated, severed. The old associations having been lopped off. No whiff or romanticism here. And yet I feel something under the posturing, some kind of earnestness that seems profoundly familiar. As if, by squinting into the future, we had seen such poetry occurring.

Where at first I felt lost facing lines such as "sense of the Infinite/ an image obtains a moss," I quickly became excited. "An image obtains a moss," is an unusual construction, but it is very clear too and not stagnant. I am reminded of the pompous American who liked to eat and produce words at an alarming rate and was quite full of herself. Gibberish, yes, but not without intelligence. Made me feel seasick to read her, as if suddenly I was floating high above, looking down at my ridiculous, grounded self.

‡ Wednesday, December 17, 2008
Upon reading a recent poem in a magazine she reognizes the difference between imaginative lyric poetry and what is purported not to be real poetry

As long as the title is clearly connected to the mid-section of the poem. As long as the eating of people is clearly a metaphor. As long as the idea of human longing is signalled early, best in the first stanza. As long as the question "What do you love?" appears. As long as there is a sense of "teasing" disunity, not too teasing though. As long as "My" and "I" appear with minimal irony. As long as the reader is constantly reminded they are human, their longing is human, and given a glass of wine, a Rusty Nail, anything in stemware, they will be fine by the end of the poem. As long as intestines aren't the end of the poem. As long as we don't spend too long on illness. As long as the doctor's appearance is not expressly for the speaker of the poem, rather say, for a brother. As long as their aren't too many specific contemporary cultural references (after all, the poem is a transporter not a mirror). As long as abstract ideas are minimal. As long as metaphor is present and doesn't stretch the imagination too far. As long as God appears (or his intestine) and at least one exclamation mark. As long as the poem ties everything together in the end. As long as there is only a residue of thinking after the event of the poem. As long as the wonder lasts only as long as turning the page. As long as it contains the word "miracles" and better if it ends there. Yes, best if it ends there.

‡ Friday, December 19, 2008
Avant Lyric, a few observations toward an essay,

Anyone who has read the anthology of Canadian poetry I edited a few years back, or has read this blog, must know how much I love lyric poetry. They might also know that I love avant-garde poetry, and L=A=N=G=U=A=G=E poetry, sound poetry, visual and concrete poetry, formal and even new formalist poetry.

In short, this blog loves poetry. Not one version of poetry, not my version, or my mentor's version – if I had such a thing – no, I love poetry, or poetries. Multiple.

So what's the problem with avant lyric then? Why am I giving these particular poets such a hard time? If my perspective is all open and inclusive, what's the big deal? A good question. It is, perhaps, not the poetry itself (though upon a closer reading there are some issues there), but the way we talk about it; the way we publish or don't publish, what we include in categories – categories in fact are bothersome, categories that make modes of writing exclusive, that brand one person as accessible and others not.

Why, for instance, is someone like Michael Dickman, published three times in the *New Yorker* this year, accessible, and someone like Katie Degentesh or K Silem Mohammad, not? My problem is with the equations that keep some poets out of publishing circles and some poets in.

There is likely a more rhizomatic way of thinking about and discussing poetry. There are connective aspects to the craft...and there are huge blocks about what the general public can or can not understand. And there is, of course, the Steinian obvervation that original is ugly and then others make it beautiful and accessible. Or others water down innovation. Or others "tone" it down.

There is, to my mind, a great deal being made of tone these days. People are offended by flarf, they hammer away at conceptual poetry with words such as "nonsense," "about nothing," "dead ends," and all matter of insults. They conflate conceptual poetry with conceit, with artifice. They link lyric poetry with painting and avant-garde poetry with conceptual art far too easily, far too simplistically. For evidence of this, see comment streams everywhere....

And meanwhile, there are certain poets and poetry that tend to rise above these little entanglements. Poetry that takes a little of this, or that, and goes off on its own to become somehow accessible. I'm interested in what this is. What makes this happen? I'm curious about this question of proportion. About the Michael Dickmans, and here in Canada, publications such as Jeramy Dodds' *Crabwise to the Hounds*, for example, a highly enjoyable, well crafted book. That is, a wonderful stream of energetic images, questions, fragmented and yet thematically linked statements, bits of artifact and archival materials that document, gesture toward essay, toward catalogue, and not so much collage as work up a kind of temporary psychological, or intellectual duststorm, a kinetic event that seems for a moment solid.

What is it about this avant lyric poetry that makes it so much more palatable than other contemporary modes? Take, for instance Kate Hall's "Little Essay on Genetics" and "The Shipping Container." Here are two poems that tend to "sound" more like prose poems than they look. Very quickly you get the voice, a quirky, inquiring perspective. You also get a sense of the kinds of tropes that appear frequently — even in the small sampling that I found after reading "Suspended." As we see here:

> It's true, the container

> has great aesthetic value but I was really hoping
> for a free watch with a rechargeable battery or
> at least a better kind of nothingness.

Read as a prose line, I'm quite content with such a line, but, but, but, what makes this poetry? And what makes this more coherent somehow than the flarf texts?

The text made me question (and requestion) my desire for a kind of polish that I don't ultimately believe in so much anymore. At least not in theory. The rough edges, the emphasis on the thinkingness of the text rather than its polish, those aspects speak to my current interests. I'm not sure I want a poem to tell me how to feel or what to think. I'm quite tired of poems that tuck everything in neatly in the end. Poems that don't recognize the world they are being carved out of. And in terms of the poem on the page, I found the actual layout, the presence of the poem on the page, to be both compelling and slightly irritating – a retrofitting of a kind of poetry that exists elsewhere in rangier forms. And gangly references to more conventional aspects of poetry. Why line breaks if one isn't going to do something with them?

But line breaks are not what this chapbook is about, and it is a random event that these questions are being tagged on Hall's chapbook, because they are questions that have lingered in my reading for some time. And the irritation stems, perhaps, from the fact that they are sufficiently accentuated to notice the dissonance of them but for no apparent reason. Why? A poet like Anne Carson is very, very attuned to how things are laid out on the page. Even *Short Talks*, her early Brick book of short prose pieces, are meant to have space around them, and they are meant to be read as "prose poems." Her insistence on having them "not" be run on one after the other, "like a grocery list," I think she said, actually dictated the entire formatting of *Open Field*. And with good reason: the poems were formally and consciously presented on the page, fully justified, smaller margins, nothing haphazard.

Again, this is not necessarily a problem of Hall's text; it is a question of the discussion and organization of contemporary poetry and one of several questions I bring to my reading these days. One question has to do with the use of formal elements. Where and why? What are line breaks doing circa 2008? And why is there so much poetry that is not acknowledging its place on a page? This spins out into, why do so many poems seem unaware of their place in a poetic tradition, lryic or otherwise? Where are the elements of "poetry"? What is going on here? What makes this more "poetic" than the apparently less successful modes of poetry, including flarf?

The oddness of the line breaks and the lay out on the page made me look more closely, and then the closer I looked, the more the poems seemed not quite to fall apart but perhaps to seem flimsy. Yes, we have musings, and they are quirky and hold together thematically, but as Hall says in the end of her chapbook:

>...I didn't want to know
>that you could add up so many things
>and have them equal so few.

Which, going back to my little analogy of the duststorm, begs the question, what happens after the dust settles? You tell me — is there some baseline thrum under the event? Because what you have after the dust settles is all that longtime engagement not only with the ideas, the thinking itself, but the shaping of the line and the project, the well-honed craft or not.

One of the things lyric poetry does to my mind, aside from providing a kind of speaking subject or subjectivity (an entity can work, no), is to provide an anchor in the poem — an emotional and intellectual anchor. That "thing," you find yourself face to face with after the dust settles. Someone, depending on your temperament, like Anne Carson, Lisa Robertson, Karen Solie, Ken Babstock, David O'Meara, Margaret Christakos, Juliana Spahr, and perhaps even a newcomer such as Jeramy Dodds, or for that matter, Mohammad. A good poet will leave you, not alone but alone with your thoughts.

Your thoughts are your solace. Not the poem's easy placations...

The question remains, is this lyric mode doing anything different? Is it taking risks, or is it taking the foment of the innovative response to lyric and making it cozy once more? Surprising surrealism in the texts, yes, but benign collections of ideas that go...where? Is it terribly old fashioned of me to want poetry to be about something? To go somewhere? And who is to judge where it should go? Who is to judge what a reader finds meaning in?

Further, are these lines more coherent than the flarf poems? Take Mohammad's "I said to Poetry":

> poetry has died, just as easily
> as junkies who spent all their money

> on dope were killed

And later:

> of course, I love Courtney, and her essays
> have appeared in the future
> some are embellished, and some are just
> a blast furnace act for all the world to behold
>
> what a sad violent fact it is
> that poetry is just a bank or something

Indeed, it is a sad fact that poetry is "just a bank" or something. And that certain poetries are ascribed to have, or to evoke feelings, and meaning, whereas others are not. What is the difference between flarf and this avant-lyric mode? Is it social, rather than individual in the way that Ryan Fitzpatrick describes flarf, or back to the lone individual in the surreal world of self-referentiality? How can we be so unsophisticated in our reading as to not note these registers in tone? Or read them? So, I guess what this unruly rant is really all about is not so much a complaint as a query about this mode and the avant lyric in general and more precisely, where and when we talk about our reading of poetry? One must address the question of tone, yes. As Lisa Robertson points out, sincerity is rhetoric. But, perhaps more importantly, we really need to unearth and investigate these assumptions around our reading and corralling of poetry.

Vanessa said...An excellent start to conversation; prefatorily, rhetoric is also sincerity insofar as there is some thingness one is to be convinced of or eased into, like cold cars and warm woolen mittens. The nut of the problem appears to be that we are perhaps not as meaningless as the well-meaninged would make us out to be, nor as endlessly fascinating as the well-versed seem to believe. If we are now at a point where ethics and aesthetics are the same face in different light, then your query puts the question point-blank, and is there then some other fashion in which critique does not have to be cooly abject or pathetically ironized, nor sentiment enacted with a whippet's trembling self-regard.

Steve said...There may be no "outside" to rhetoric (depends what you mean by "rhetoric") but there are claims whose literal sense we believe, and other claims whose literal sense we do not believe, or would not affirm. Isn't the motor to flarf antilyrical inasmuch as flarf is satirical or sarcastic, pointed outward, towards how other people (erroneously or inevitably) see themselves and the world? Whereas lyric (avant or otherwise) comes first from how the imagined speaker (or writer or assembler, if you prefer) sees herself. Of course, these categories can overlap: the successful satirist, if she is interesting enough and self-conscious about it, shows us something of herself, which is why I like The Anger Scale, and why I like Pope's "Epistle to Dr Arbuthnot."

Vanessa said...And then isn't the point of conceptualism that there is no inside that is not outside and visa versa? To all things, they're surfaces.

Lemon Hound said...Steve, yes, I think you're right about the outward versus inward, but lyric that is inward can also refract, reflect a largeness of perspective. And your last note is really more what I would argue as a poetic quality one can identify and appreciate regardless of the aesthetic of the poem – that is lyric, language, avant lyric, etc. In other words the consciousness of the poem/poet, not a perceived sincerity.

Brenda said... Lots to think about here. The corralling of poetry. I like how you put that. So apt. The sorting, the holding pens, the gates, the dust. All the bellowing.
Steven said... The Dickman poem you link to seems very traditional. An encapsulated moment, well defined images, and very carefully done. Read it once, get it all in that reading, and while pleasurable enough to read again, no real additional challenge or fun in reading it again and again? I don't remember the poems of his that have been published in *The New Yorker* (and that I don't remember them probably says it all, in a way). There are poems that serve it right up (can be more or less fully and totally grokked the first or second time read), and poems that aren't. *The New Yorker* mostly publishes the former.

Ken Jacobs said... i know this is late but i am interested in what you mean by "apparently less successful modes of poetry" ... this question does not regard flarf but how you are measuring 'success' within this post or in general. Recognition of a 'tradition' and appropriate, informed response or distribution or something else ... it seems to me there's a distinct talking amongst themselves going on in many different 'innovative' communities ... is or can that be enough?

Lemon Hound said... the Dickman poem does seem traditional, and easily consumed. Ken, A good question. How does one measure the success of a poem? Or one's life as a poet? No one wants to admit that they have a certain path, or audience in mind, but most of us do. That might be one way to measure. Many people think appearing in *Poetry Magazine* is a sign of success. Even people who should know better than to allow such a small aperture to define anything. Meanwhile there are many poets that don't get discussed, or discussed enough – as diverse in range and aesthetics as, here in Canada for instance, Don Coles or David O'Meara, M. Nourbese Philip or Margaret Christakos.

Ken said...lh, i really like what you got to say here ... really ... just found this blog via "think again." m. wallace links to you. what i am interested in is that you have defined lots of criteria above. and there are flarfists who are very successful at these things – k. mohammad & rod smith come to mind & bill louma but they are never going to be read or heard outside of a small community ... i would never measure their work as "less successful" because of that since amongst those who measure with the type of criteria you mention, a small community, their "poems" are measured as such. this borders on sounding like silliman talking about the early days of langpo but i am willing to risk the comparison. (old worn out arguments, i suppose) i will read on. very glad to have been introduced to your blog.

Paul Vermeersch said...lh, you ask, "Is it terribly old fashioned of me to want poetry to be about something?" I believe the answer is "No." No matter how "innovative" people seem to be in finding new ways to (not) write, there will always be satisfaction to be taken in a composition that is well-written. Poetry is maybe our oldest art form. If the idea of well-crafted words was even capable of being passe, it would not have lasted through the past 10,000 years of human endeavour. We would have no poems, no books to speak of. The ability of language to inspire, frighten, entertain, sadden, inform, manipulate or otherwise move or transform an audience is fundamental to the human animal. The world constantly changes. New ideas emerge not only in poetics, but in every field of thought. New things happen. And that, at least, provides writers with something new to write about. Poetry about poetics can be mere navel-gazing, a game for a clique of initiates to play in private, but poetry about the world out there, the one we live in, about, as you say, "something" ...well, that's not old-fashioned. There's nothing wrong with wanting something to be relevant to your lived experience. In fact, I think that's what most people want from written forms of art. They want to be invited to understand something about the world a little better, or to be introduced to something they hadn't known before. There's nothing old fashioned about that. Interesting ideas. I look forward to seeing where you might take this line of thinking in the future.

Lemon Hound said...Ken, You point out that some flarf is more successful, "k. mohammad & rod smith," for example, yet even they "are never going to be read or heard outside of a small community..." That's exactly the problem. To shift to the world of sports briefly, imagine sports coverage that was only one sport? Imagine commentators who only knew the rules of hockey, or baseball? Imagine a sports section that only discussed football, and with the tone that suggested, of course, there is only football... It seems to me that this is what we face as poets. There are too few able to see the entire field of poetry. There is a larger picture, to use yet another cheesy analogy...

Lemon Hound said...Paul, I agree, but as per my previous response, who is to judge what is new? What is successful? What is meaningful? If our editors are unable to assess new forms of poetry, to draw connections between what a particular poet is doing now and how that work might fit into the larger, more wonderfully complex world of poetry, then who will? All art needs to have context, to have discussions built up around it. Not dissection: discussion.

Paul said... "Not dissection: discussion." You nailed it there, LH. Unfortunately, the current prevailing winds of academic criticism tend toward dissection rather than discussion, toward an attitude that is hostile to literature, an attitude that seeks in invalidate literature or exploit it for a single discipline-specific (i.e. "teachable") attribute, rather than explore the fullness and inimitable complexity of a work. Hopefully, this will change in time, because it creates an environment for a particularly poisonous poetic ecology. As long as these ever-narrower kinds of literary scholarship are encouraged, those that relegate the literature they study to the rank of secondary text behind the criticism itself, where the function of literature is reduced to little more than support material for the critical theory, then ever-narrower forms of literature will evolve in the hopes of fitting into these thin, discipline-specific niches, and along the way, proponents of these niche-poetics will loudly declare that everything that came before is now obsolete, making the kind of broad-spectrum discussion (rather than dissection) that you yearn for somewhat difficult.

Lemon Hound said...Paul, here's to discussion and complexity, yes, yes, yes. But it isn't only academics that engage in this behaviour, reviewers, publishers, editors and poets themselves also indulge. As one poet emailed me recently to say, "you know before publication which books will be reviewed where and who by. There are few surprises in poetry circles..." I say more surprises please. Particularly as review space shrinks. Good surprises tho, thoughtful ones, not the nasty kind.

ken said...as k. mohammad in a blog entry once put ... s. plath is a gateway drug ... it is a very rare beast who gets to lisa jarnot or lisa robertson (very visible poets) or kevin davies via jackson mac low... i am not sure it is productive to expect it... that said, this perhaps doesn't address channels of dissemination, though isn't niche part of the complexity? aren't those who speak in narrow bands contributors to this debate? what make this blog & discussion possible? who can take k. goldsmith's assertions as to what is "contemporary" as anything but absurd!? i mean obsolescence is so last century.

Paul said...Niches are fine, yes, and necessary. Niches, alcoves, offshoots, branches, sidestreets, tributaries, all sorts of outgrowths. Makes for a good poetic gene pool, puts more poetry tools in the poetry toolbox. But when a tributary cuts itself off from the source river, it will dry up very quickly. And once you learn to use a saw, that doesn't mean you'll never need to use a hammer again. If poets write a poem that intends to be difficult, adversarial, inpenetrable, condescending, or abstruse, they shouldn't be surprised that few people will take the time to read it, even those who do "get" it.

ken said...agreed... if they are writing to a niche they shouldn't expect any response outside of that niche. that is, well, pathological. for those who can or are willing to keep their interests in many pots and can even work in many modes, to expect more "difficult" or abstruse poems to be integrated easily into the main paths of dissemination seems to me absurd.

Lemon Hound said...Paul: "If poets write a poem that intends to be difficult, adversarial, inpenetrable, condescending, or abstruse, they shouldn't be surprised that few people will take the time to read it, even those who do 'get' it." Thank god poets write against this kind of thinking...otherwise there would be no Donne, no Hopkins, no Blake, no Whitman, no Stein, no Dennis Lee, no Paul Celan, and so on, and so on, and so on... Many, many, many, many, many, many people take the time to read "difficult" poetry all the time. It's what makes us grow. Okay, I'm unplugging –

‡ AN AFTERWORD:
Looking At Looking Through

Paysage is a word for looking at as much as a word for looking through. Just as it directly refers to a scene or landscape, it also conjures its own oblique representation via the interpretive act in play – *paysage riant, agréable paysage, tableau de paysage, paysage à la gouache*. In my broken clay pot version of English, therein lies its broad considered attention, attention paid to the paying of attention. The blog entries collected in *Unleashed* similarly circle around points of attention, sometimes geographic, sometimes polemic, sometimes historic, sometimes comic, always aesthetic, always poetic. Like a good and slightly crabby paramour, Queyras insists on the engagement of herself and others and herself with others. The art she likes, she writes about. The art she doesn't, she writes at. Her thoughts come as her countrymen call them – "thots" – snaps of keen consciousness. She provides tips for her readers, things to do, things to chew on. Books to read, to throw across the room. She rebukes herself and others when attention falters or when ontology is not what it's cracked up to be. She's not a feminist, not really, but Really, because she believes to her smallest bones that people are not simply translations of Abide By Me. Nor is she an environmentalist of the t-shirt and boutique tea variety, but the kind who stands bluntly before the outdoors, Romantic in a way that we should be, if we only could wear hats without thinking, if we could simply be as we are prone to being, both towering and cowed, like Friedrich's *Wanderer above the Sea of Fog*, or, to cop another kind of lyric feel, "fostered alike by beauty and fear."

Photographs arrest Queyras, tropes rankle and possess. She has serial fascinations: Lisa Robertson, Erín Moure, Jeff Wall, Christian Bök, Andreas Gursky, Robert Smithson, Samuel

Beckett, Gertrude Stein. Virginia Woolf. She's a self-confessed creature of the Canadian West, where vistas spread wide as the rivers they cradle and the ladies they bed. Perhaps, it is the lure and threat of the open spaces that serve to spark and burr her interest in big art, big pictures and bigger conversation. She likes photos you can walk in, poems that never fully end. Like a perpetual Vladimir, she wants the back and forth while keeping on the ongoing that moves towards an ever-receding horizon. The point of the ever-receding horizon is the horizon: to aim at that which cannot be captured but only be sought in the now (not the Now) is to demand a kind of excruciating infinity, to dedicate oneself to the constancy of the moonlit, the sunlit, the desperate.

Formally, a blog is also a kind of potentially endless witness bearing. Having no natural terminus, it also has no set bandwidth, and entries can drop like pennies into the slotted ether, or can dilate into another conversation, or branch miasmatically out in directions beyond the direction of its instigator. To this end, *Unleashed,* the book, includes entries in which the authorial I is ricocheting off comments outside the space of this bound project. This brings Realism and Romanticism into virtual discourse ("into" as in incorporate, not its lazier cousin, overlay) with discourse itself. For rather than using her blog as a hyacinth-strewn pool, Queyras turns it to salon-prompt (to be read is reading in the futur imparfait). By the same token, she posts some of her own poems, but not so very many, and not so very owned. She prefers to enlist other poets to comment on other forms of poetry, including the poetry of the youtube clip or the rouge interview, and she delights in all manner of exegesistic fencing.

Queyras likes to literally (sic) snapshot herself as a shadow of herself set against the backdrop of whatever foreground she finds herself in (sich). In the excess text of the blog/world, our voices are the too/much of the too/many. And yet our comments are contagious, our poetries puny and persistent. And still we will stop to comment, typing with the determination of bank officers, reading with the faith of gleaners at sunrise. Putting even our blog posts into something as permanent as paper, as perfect/bound as perfect bound. So that for all her forays, Queyras is no flâneur, for the flâneur is man as mote, wisping through the boulevards, resplendent in his fragile, muff/driven decay. Rather, like the loosed hound, Queyras paws at this and that, sniffs deeply, mouths what she will, roots in the bracken and startles all the birds, and then stops, and points at things shot/worthy.

Vanessa Place
Los Angeles
October 2009

‡ Colophon

Manufactured in an edition of 500 copies in the fall of 2009 by BookThug | Distributed in Canada by The Literary Press Group of Canada www.lpg.ca | Distributed in the United States by Small Press Distribution www.spdbooks.org | Shop on-line at www.bookthug.ca

BOOK
PRODUCTION
WAR ECONOMY
STANDARD

Type + Design by Jay MillAr
The Department of Critical Thought
   is edited for the press by Kate Eichhorn.